CLASSIC CONVERSATIONS AND R&B

'90s HIP HOP AND R&B

BARRY KRUTCHIK

Classic Conversations: "'90s Hip Hop and R&B"
© 2025 Barry Krutchik
All rights reserved. No part of this book may be reproduced, stored in a retrieval system, or transmitted in any form or by any means—electronic, mechanical, photocopying, recording, or otherwise—without the prior written permission of the publisher.

Published by: Krutchie Entertainment

Author: Barry Krutchik

Editor: Jermaine Johnson II

Additional Editorial Assistance: Petra Wolf

Art Director: David Gerhard, MFA

Cover Design: Robert Fisher

Cassette Design: Gary Adler

This book is a work of nonfiction. Every effort has been made to provide accurate information. However, the author and publisher assume no responsibility for errors, omissions, or contrary interpretations.

ISBN: 979-8-9928899-1-8

Printed in the United States of America

I dedicate this book to all the artists who not only gave me a soundtrack to my life, but also for spending time with me, laughing with me, sharing their experiences with me. It's been a wild ride.

ACKNOWLEDGEMENTS

I want to start off by acknowledging my dead parents. Sorry, that's my humor. They're still dead, but they're very much a part of my life and more specifically, this book. How so, you ask? I didn't realize until I started this project how much of my upbringing led me to this career.

My mother made sure from birth that music, television, & film played a crucial role in my social calendar. She took me to the theater, but I didn't gravitate towards it-still don't. She encouraged participation in "the arts," didn't gravitate towards that either-sports was my first choice. We watched television and movies as a family, but music was the breakthrough. I loved it, she knew it, and she encouraged me to play an instrument. She was not thrilled that I chose the drums-I guess I liked loud.

Mom was the type of woman who would watch the Oscars while talking on the phone to her sister in another state so they could discuss, enjoy, and critique the show together. She loved movies so much that for my thirteenth birthday, she took me and a dozen of my friends to Skylake Mall in North Miami Beach to see the R-rated film *The Warriors.* The box office rep wouldn't allow this, and I watched my mother explain that she spoke to every one of my friends' parents and got permission to do so. Of course she didn't, I watched her lie right in front of me-she's a quick thinking genius. But it worked, and we got to see *The Warriors* "come out and play." It was one of my favorite birthdays ever, not to mention that my mother also smuggled in candy for everybody.

As far as my father, he just always told me to "have fun." Part of me wishes he told me to get a job that guaranteed financial stability. He knew that life was short and that "fun" was a necessity for your health. There's something to be said about "being happy," or at least acting like you're happy. This is way before "free your mind and the rest will follow" as well as vision boards and "The Secret."

Digesting entertainment from day one IS "having fun." It has the power to facilitate happiness, and sorrow. I remember the time I interviewed the legendary Willie Dixon for the Rhythm & Blues Foundation, and I asked the guitar great about the blues being a "sad music." He corrected me, "the blues ain't a sad music, it's a glad music." He could see the perplexed look on my face, so he went on to explain that "life is like a roller coaster, there's going to be ups and downs but you just have to remember to enjoy the ride." And what a ride it's been.

I'd like to acknowledge and thank Melinda Ruben, who I met via phone on my first day in Los Angeles. She had a cool job where she went to concerts and movies for free, and got to interview famous people. Sign me up! She told me about a similar gig at a small production company called L.E.G. Productions, where I met my eventual boss and unofficial west coast mother Laura Gross. She was already a veteran of the broadcast industry, and she taught me how to book, conduct, edit, and utilize a proper interview. Through

Laura and her L.E.G. clients, I was able to learn and interview many of the biggest names in entertainment for all mediums— print, radio & television. I reconnected with Laura years later, and she gave me access to many of my old interviews which was a tremendous walk down pop culture memory lane. I thank you Laura.

With booking and interviewing under my belt, I made the jump to Premiere Radio which was the production arm of what is now iHeartMedia. Thanks to Steve Lehman, Kraig Kitchin and my entire radio family. Oh the stories! That's another book.

I'd like to acknowledge my daughter Maya and my Queen Amy. They've been beyond supportive, cheerleading this project from day one. They think it's cool.

I'd like to acknowledge Howard Stern for being smart (me), funny (me), not the best looking (apparently me) and for being a creative genius on the radio. Thank you Howard, and congrats on your third book *Howard Stern Comes Again* which shines a light on dozens of interviews over his career, inserting transcripts and fresh takes with reasons for inclusion in the book. What a great idea. If only I could do something similar. Yes King, I thank you.

INTRODUCTION

If I had a nickel for every time someone told me to write a book, I'd have about $2. Don't do the math. The point is—I've lived a colorful life around fascinating people, and apparently, that means I have a story to tell.

They're right. But sharing my life with others has never come easy. I've always been the guy behind the scenes—behind the mic, behind the camera. I liked it that way. Shining the spotlight on myself? Hard to digest. Ironically, for the people I work with, that spotlight is their oxygen.

Even today, I struggle to explain what I do for a living. It's been a running joke among my friends—most of whom still have no clue. But for the purposes of this book, here's my short story.

After a brief stint in the marketing department of the legendary music industry trade Hits Magazine, I landed a gig interviewing recording artists and actors, mainly for syndicated radio. I wrote the scripts for countdown shows—so if you ever heard a DJ say, "Coming in at number 20, it's Mary J. Blige with 'I Can Love You'"—then play a clip of Mary talking about the song before the track hit the airwaves? Yeah, I had something to do with that.

In reality, that moment started with me sitting in a hotel room at the Four Seasons in Beverly Hills on March 4, 1997, setting up a mic and a tape deck, asking Mary J. Blige about her album (and everything else). Every week, when one of her songs was on the charts, I had to write an intro, choose the right soundbite, and craft the perfect outro. Sounds simple, right?

I was doing this nonstop, churning out interviews across every format, covering everyone from recording artists to movie stars, game show hosts to sports legends.

A sample day in my life?

Morning interview with the Bee Gees at the Sunset Marquis.

Drive down Sunset Boulevard to Capitol Records to chat with the Red Hot Chili Peppers.

Head over the hill to Warner Bros. in Burbank to interview Matthew Perry on the set of *Friends*.

Cap it all off with an Earth, Wind & Fire concert at the Pantages Theatre.

I was putting in my 10,000 hours—and I started getting good at my craft.

> I realized early on that I might be the eighth journalist an artist is talking to that day. They were exhausted, hearing the same questions over and over. So I made it fun—for them, and for me.

I wasn't the first person to ask Babyface about his songwriting process. But there's a way to do it with humor:

"Hey **Face**, here's a question you've **never** heard before... What's your creative process?"

He'd laugh. And then, I'd get gold.

Fast forward to 2020—the pandemic. Stuck at home, I started digitizing my old interviews from the '90s. I played them in the background while working. And something hit me.

These weren't just interviews. They were a time capsule.

I had been inside the room when pop culture was shifting. Many of the artists I interviewed were debuting at the time. Now, 30 years later, they're icons. And listening back? The interviews were really entertaining—kind of like podcasting before podcasting.

There were no boundaries, no formats. Some conversations were ten minutes. Others lasted over an hour. Don't worry, I've edited for brevity and flow, but every word you'll read in this book was spoken—so yes, expect some repeated phrases and the occasional "you know." That's what makes them real.

I interviewed legends across music, film, sports, and comedy:

Pop culture icons: *Bob Hope, Mel Brooks, Norman Lear, Sidney Poitier, Jim Henson, Oprah Winfrey, Bill Cosby*

Comedy legends: *Eddie Murphy, George Carlin, Steve Martin, Jim Carrey, Dave Chappelle, Dan Aykroyd, John Candy*

Sports legends: *Magic Johnson, Sugar Ray Leonard, Billie Jean King, Gale Sayers, Martina Navratilova*

Music legends: *Stevie Wonder, Whitney Houston, Isaac Hayes, Chaka Khan, The Eagles, Van Halen, Linda Ronstadt, Bonnie Raitt, Beastie Boys, Duran Duran, Lenny Kravitz, KISS, Usher, and many more.*

SO WHY CHOOSE '90S HIP HOP & R&B?

Having spent 20+ years with Black Entertainment Television, I felt my pimp hand was strong enough to take on one of my favorite genres. Not to mention, I was often the "white guy" at '90s album listening parties—whoops, said that out loud. But it's true.

Picking which artists to feature wasn't easy. Should I go with my favorites, the biggest stars, or the most controversial voices? In the end, I chose a mix of all three.

Boyz II Men and TLC? Undeniably the biggest male and female R&B groups of the '90s. Also two of my personal favorites. That's not to say I didn't love talking to En Vogue, New Edition, SWV, Jodeci, Xscape, 112, Blackstreet, Silk, Jagged Edge, 702, Total, Dru Hill, Blaque, Shai, Color Me Badd, Brownstone, and many more. They were great!

For solo R&B acts, Aaliyah and Toni Braxton were no-brainers. R. Kelly (yeah, I know) had more Top 40 hits than any other male solo artist in the '90s. And while Luther Vandross is often associated with the '80s, his first Grammy came in 1991, so he made the cut. Plus, he was one of my favorite interviews—and humans—of all time.

On the Hip Hop side, starting with Vanilla Ice and ending with Jay-Z felt like the perfect career arc, with legends like MC Hammer, LL Cool J, Will Smith, and Missy Elliott rounding things out.

Every artist featured in this book played a role in my life. Their talent, ambition, and resilience remind us why the '90s were more than just a golden age of music. Their stories are a part of my classic conversations.

"WHO IS THE 'WHITE GUY' IN THE ROOM?" ME. THIS TIME AT ONE OF MY HIP HOP AND R&B EVENTS."

Photo: Bobby Quillard

FOREWORD: "BARRY WHITE"

VANILLA ICE: THE ICEMAN RAPPETH
December 8, 1990

BOYZ II MEN: MOTOWN PHILLY VEGAS
November 18, 1991

TLC: CRAZY SEXY FUN
February 28, 1992

R. KELLY: AGE AIN'T NOTHING BUT A NUMBER
March 13, 1992

TONI BRAXTON: DYN-O-MITE
September 4, 1992

WILL SMITH: CODE RED
December 11, 1993

MC HAMMER: A FUNKY HEADHUNTER
February 10, 1994

AALIYAH: ONE IN A MILLION
May 5, 1994

LUTHER VANDROSS: RONZONI SONO BUONI IS SO GOOD
February 16, 1995

LL COOL J: WALKING WITH A PANTHER…TO ROSCOE'S
January 11, 1996

MISSY ELLIOTT: SUPA DUPA ORIGINAL
February 17, 1998

JAY-Z: MY FIRST, MY LAST, MY EVERYTHING
January 7, 2000

FOREWORD BY BARRY WHITE...
IF HE WAS STILL ALIVE

I don't think I've ever written or been asked to write a foreword for a book…and honestly, I would never do one if I were alive. But I am not, so if I was going to do one, it would be for Barry Krutchik, or as I used to call him, "Little B". There were 3 days in my life that I remember clearly, October 6, 1989, October 25, 1991, and September 26, 1994. Each of those days was spent with Little B. I was recording for A & M records at the time, going through the usual promotional vehicles, one of which being the dreaded back-to-back interviews on the lot. In 1989, I released *The Man Is Back!*, my self-produced seventeenth album, the "comeback album" as some people called it. 'Don't call it a comeback, I've been here for years, I'm rockin' my peers, puttin' suckers in fear, makin' the tears rain down like a monsoon, listen to the bass go boom.' Okay, a little hip hop joke with lyrics courtesy of LL Cool J. Moving forward on the foreword.

I remember the first time I met Little B. He wasn't the usual music journalist. First of all, he was young. And, he was white. Hmmmm….Who is this kid? Did he know his shit? Did he prep this interview? Did he know who he was messing with? Well, let me just say that this kid came correct. He did his homework, he knew the music, he threw some softballs and as an artist, I hit those pitches like a veteran being inducted into the Hall of Fame. Bam!

But here's the thing...his enthusiasm for the interview, hanging onto every answer I gave, and following whatever tangent or curveball I threw at him made it enjoyable for both of us. And he was funny, and I like to laugh. So after our debut interview, I remember feeling that I'm going to be okay, this project will be okay. And then I exhaled.

Two years later, I am releasing *Put Me In Your Mix*, an album that critics felt was a return to my sultry ballads...the public not so much. The publicity team put me in a room and lined up back-to-back interviews for the day. After a few journalists came to ask me the usual questions, next up was Little B. Are you kidding me? I forgot about him from the last record, but bam, here he was...same kid, still young, still white, and still eager to talk music and promote the album. Damn that was fun. And then I exhaled.

It took a few more years before I decided to make music again, but when you've been told you're the "Icon Of Love" for many years, you should listen to your people and embrace it. I did, and made an album. I had a press day at the A & M Records lot on La Brea Ave in Hollywood. Since I am still dead, I want to say that the A & M lot was a creative space, a unique space, a space with history-it used to be home to Charlie Chaplin studios from 1918 to 1953. After A & M records, it became home to another legendary creator and his estate, Jim Henson of Sesame Street fame. Fun fact, the creatives (Jim) and his Cookie Monster and The Crumbs Unlimited Orchestra sang a parody of my song "I'm Going to Love You Just a Little More Baby" in 1981. It was called "Me Going To Munch You." True story. And just before publishing this book, musician John Mayer and director McG apparently have purchased the famed creative space but I digress. Moving forward on the foreword.

So I am about to promote my *Icon of Love* album in 1994, with multiple interviews and in walks Little B…I can't tell you how happy that made me feel. I finally felt like I had a solid album (production credits from Gerald Levert as well as Jimmy Jam & Terry Lewis), and then I get to see Little B and laugh!?!? What is it my birthday? It was 2 weeks earlier. This was my favorite interview of the day because it wasn't an interview, it was old friends getting together and having a conversation. Or as Little B would now say, a "classic conversation".

I hope you enjoy his interviews, and his "conversations" with '90s Hip Hop and R&B stars. I guarantee these artists enjoyed talking to Little B.

Editor's note: Just want to be clear, Barry White didn't actually write this foreword. This was the author Barry Krutchik having fun and honoring the memory of an artist he really enjoyed knowing and working with.

AN EXCLUSIVE HITS INTERVIEW WITH
VANILLA ICE BY BARRY KRUTCHIK

THE ICEMAN RAPPETH

Whether he's hip-hop's answer to Elvis Presley or Pat Boone, Vanilla Ice is the hottest debut artist in years and the man who's making rap a household word in suburban malls and homes across this great land of ours. The Iceman has been melting hearts by the millions, seven going on eight to be exact, since his SBK Records debut album, "To The Extreme," hit the stores last September. Spurred on by the success of the #1 single, "Ice Ice Baby," the rapper with the weird brows had nothing better to do than to take time out for an interview on a Saturday afternoon. In the hotel lobby, Chill, one of Ice's bodyguards, led me up to the interview suite. My first impression of the Cool One was that of a young streetkid suddenly vaulted into superstardom out of nowhere. During our 60-minute session — taped by Ice's own people lest he be misquoted— Van the man did nothing to dispell that impression, though he did feel the need to clear the air regarding the recent negative publicity about his fabricated past. If you can look past the bum rap, you'll find a fun-loving 22-year-old who is living out what must be everybody's rock dream-come-true. After the interview, Ice and I decided to play some hoops. Since we were ball-less [*Ed. note: No kidding...*], we picked up and headed to the mall with Chill and his road manager to do some quick shopping. After politely dodging autograph-seekers, we ended up at the jewelry store, where Ice did some serious purchasing, spending as much on baubles as you would on a mid-priced automobile. Ah, to be young, rich and famous. As long as you don't get drafted. Precisely the dilemma faced by HITS' ex-basement correspondent and battle-fatigued veteran Barry "As Funny As A Rubber" Krutchik.

HITS February 4, 1991

YOU ALWAYS REMEMBER YOUR FIRST... COVER ARTICLE.

VANILLA ICE WAS A POLARIZING FIGURE IN POP CULTURE - BEFORE ANYONE WAS TALKING OF CULTURAL MISAPPROPRIATION.

In 1990, you could not escape him or his music; the ubiquitous rapper ruled the charts and the conversations of music lovers, critics, and fans alike. "Ice Ice Baby" was an anthem, the first hip hop single to top the Billboard charts—I'm not counting Blondie's "Rapture" as it was a pop song with rap elements. It's credited for introducing hip hop to a mainstream audience. Back then, "mainstream" was code for "white." It still may be but the reality was that there were only three other white rappers around at the time and they were all in the same group (Beastie Boys). I'm not saying there would be no Eminem without a Robert Van Winkle (aka Ice), I'm just saying he was HUGE and getting the interview was sort of a career milestone for me. Let me explain...

I was writing scripts for syndicated pop radio shows at the time, so having audio of the artist talking about their music every week was crucial. And Ice could talk—content was never a problem so I edited down our conversation to the juiciest parts. In fact, this was the first—and only—time an artist had his own tape machine to record the interview himself, "lest he be misquoted." He felt the press had been too harsh on him, but I wasn't like other critics. I wasn't the type to prefer talking about underground artists who rarely made it onto radio because their music was "too commercial."

I'm not saying his debut album, *To The Extreme*, was a masterpiece—far from it. But Ice's popularity was undeniable, and I saw an opportunity to capitalize on my interview. I pitched the story to Hits Magazine and landeed my first cover: *The Iceman Rappeth*. Funny, right? Oh, and I also got a $200 check, which—let's be honest—is reason enough to consider this conversation a classic.

BK: There's a lot going on these days for you. I mean, you're on every magazine. Did you expect any of this, and how are you handling it?

ICE: I'm handling it day by day [chuckles]. A lot of business out here, man. When you got all the time in the world, you wish you had all the money in the world. When you got all the money in the world, you wish you had all the time in the world.

You know, I used to think, "Stars got it made—all the girls and money. That's all." Yeah, right. Believe that! All you do is work—24/7, man. You work constantly. I mean, you seriously work for your money. You got people that complain about nine-to-fives and stuff like that? Take on the life of a star, and you'll see what I'm talking about. It's not nine-to-five, it's 24/7.

BK: Have you noticed the change in yourself?

ICE: Oh, hell yeah. As far as being myself? I mean,

I'm still the same old Robbie Van Winkle—you know, from the streets, just kicking it.

But my lifestyle now? Completely flipped. I have a totally different lifestyle. I mean, I'm not at home. I haven't seen home in so long, it's pathetic. And, you know, I've been there all my life, and now I'm just never there.

It's incredible, man. My lifestyle has completely changed.

BK: What was so special about Ice Ice Baby? Why do you think it—

ICE: Different style. It's more catchy. It gets you thinking—first time you hear it, you go home and you're [rapping] "ding ding ding da da ding ding." You go [singing the hook] "Ice Ice Baby." It's just real catchy, and the lyrics aren't something like—you can't understand. You can understand the lyrics real clear. And it's just—the whole thing is a real catchy tune.

Now, you know, other rappers, they want to come out and diss me because of stuff like that. But, you know, it's the biggest joke, because I can sit here all day long and write battle rhymes—"I'm this, and I'm bad, and I'm this, you know, and I'm the best" and all this stuff—I can write that all day. But like I say, it ain't gonna sell.

And, you know, I went six times platinum yesterday. So, you know, all I got to say to people that want to diss me is—take it to the bank. [laughs]

BK: I just want to stop and say 6 million, that's hot.

> I said "that's hot" way before Paris Hilton did, maybe she got her catch phrase from me?

BK: I just interviewed Bobby Vinton yesterday—he's from the '60s, had like seven #1s. The reason I'm mentioning him is because he said, *"There's nothing like a #1."*

ICE: There isn't. Second place can't touch number one. There's nothing like a number one record—it's the feeling, man. And once you get it, it's a dream come true. You know, it's the hardest thing to do, but yet, the easiest thing to do is have a number one record. It's just incredible. Out of all the people in the world, there's only one number one.

BK: Got that right. What is your creative process? Is there some sort of routine you go through when a song comes to you?

ICE: Just when I sit down—I'll get in the mood to write a song. And I'll sit down and think about what I want to write about.

And when I'm in a real good mood, feeling like writing, then I'll sit down and write two, three, four songs at once. I'll start on one idea, then halfway through the song, I'll think of another idea. So I'll just set that aside and start on another song. Then halfway through that—or after the first verse—I'll say, *"Oh man, I just thought of another rhyme."*

And I'll go, *"Hold up, that won't fit this one,"* but I'll start another one. Then I'll go back to those and complete them. I'll come back to them days later—next time I go, *"Hmm, yeah."* Then I'll write and make a second verse. And then I'll stop on that second verse, like, *"Oh, this is something cool that fits this other song."*

I'm working on three, four songs at the same time—all just coming off the top of my head, based on what I'm thinking about at the moment.

BK: How do you decide what gets sampled and what doesn't? I mean, like, are these songs that you've dug growing up?

ICE: No, I never listened, it's before my time actually, my

brother had records that I went through, and you know, he had them and stuff. I grew up listening to James Brown and Parliament Funkadelic, stuff like that. And since the seventh grade is when I've been rapping, and that's when "Rapper's Delight" came out Sugarhill Gang. And so you know, I've been jamming all that stuff. My brother got into the other side of it. And that's kind of where I got a little edge over some people because I can get, you know, both tastes of it. And I can put some old, the new stuff, there's no way you could sample any new rock and roll but the old rock and roll kind of had a beat to it, you know, kind of danceable rock and roll and nowadays rock and roll was like, [imitates guitar solo] you know, like whoa, slow down. But you know, yeah, and you can put it with a hip hop beat and it's like [Ice starts beatboxing].

> I'm used to artists singing in an interview, but looking back, he may have been the only artist to beatbox.

ICE: And you know, and you can just [Ice mimicking the Queen/Bowie sampled hook] "ding ding ding dada ding ding." I also got some stuff coming out. I got a song, I'm doing "Satisfaction" with the Rolling Stones. I'm doing it with them, Mick Jagger, all of them. They called us and they said, "Hey, we want you to do a song". …I did a rap song "Satisfaction" a long time ago, and we were gonna put it on this album, but they denied it. Now they call us back since they see what we're doing. And we got a number one record. And they say, hey, we want to do it with them.

BK: Working with The Stones, that would be something to look forward to.

ICE: It's gonna be great. It's gonna be real great.

> I've heard the song and it wasn't great. But I love this story because at the time, this was a news item. Ice wanted to use the sample, The Stones denied the request, but after the success of his debut, the band came back and said "Yeah, we love your creative approach to music, and think you're good enough to sample our music." I'm paraphrasing here for "we gonna make a lot of money."

BK: How is Ice in the studio—Vanilla Ice in the studio?

ICE: I learned all hands-on, man. At home, I learned—you know, I got the drum machines, I program them and all that stuff, and my DJ, Earthquake, helped me learn how to do it. And I got down to doing it and started producing, man.

I produce my own stuff, you know? That's one thing that's incredible, because I don't have any big-time producer behind me. I got me—and I got a number one record—so I guess that automatically makes me a big producer too. So, you know, that makes me feel good, but...

BK: How hard have you worked?

ICE: Oh, I worked extremely hard. I've struggled. I was penniless, man. I was broke my whole entire life until six, seven months ago, because I didn't have anything, man. I couldn't even pay for the gas in my car. I couldn't even pay for the car—it was about to get repossessed. As a matter of fact, now? Just bought me a new car. Bought that car off. Bought my new house—and the other new house. I mean, I'm not bragging, I'm just saying, you know, it helps me a lot.

God came through for me, that's for sure.

BK: It's kind of like living your dreams.

ICE: Oh, it's definitely a dream come true. There's no doubt about it. I'm living my dream. But it's a living fact that your dreams can come true. You just got to want them bad enough. And that's what I did. I wanted it bad enough. I stuck with it, didn't die, man. I mean, for three years. We were struggling hard. And we just never gave up. Yep, yep.

BK: And then being white, rapping, I mean, a lot of people make a great thing out of it. I think you know that you're doing this…

ICE: Well, that's the reason why you don't see too many other you know, white people doing it. And that's the reason why they got, they call, you know, white people who can't dance, or they say he's got the white boys disease, you know, he can't dance. And it's, it's true. The proven fact is it's true. The majority of white people cannot dance, they have no rhythm. And the reason being is because they didn't grow up like I did. And you know, being around the funk and I'm like, man, it's so easy to dance and have rhythm. Why can't you do it? You know, it just comes natural to me.

> I take a little issue with the "white people can't dance" stereotype, we all know "white people can't jump."

BK: What does the name signify?

ICE: Vanilla Ice, my complexion. You got chocolate and you got vanilla and my homeboys made it up for me, just started like any nickname would start you know. They started off, called me Vanilla. Ice didn't come on until three and a half years ago when I became professional, because I said some rhymes to some of my friends in Dallas. I say you know some rhymes and they go man that was smooth as ice, vanilla. I go, huh? They was 'That was smooth as Ice, vanilla.' I said 'Vanilla Ice'. Yeah, Vanilla Ice came about.

BK: There are so many people that are trying to do what you're doing.

ICE: It won't work.

BK: What sets you apart?

ICE: Everybody thinks you know, since there's a white guy here, there's gonna always be others. I'm gonna set the pace for a lot of other white guys come up, you know, and be big and stuff, but I don't think it's really going to happen because everybody thought that was gonna happen with the Beastie Boys too. And it didn't, you know, because rap music is still from the streets. And, there's still not very many white people growing up in the streets.

> I too am from the streets. Well, there was a cul-de-sac on my block. I got that line from Glen Phillips, the lead singer of the '90s pop rock band Toad the Wet Sprocket. I give credit when credit is due.
>
> Ice deserves credit for his success, whether he was from "the streets" or not. It doesn't matter as the kid made a hit record, and many other "white" rappers have tried to replicate the formula and there are still only a few that have become as successful in music.

ICE: You know, there's gonna be record companies that got some guy that thinks he can rap or something, and they're gonna try and put him out. But it's just not going to work because it's not my image. It's not my color that made me; it's the songs. The songs are slamming, the songs are hitting, and I did it myself. Some other white guy maybe cannot do all the things I can do because I can produce, I can write, I can choreograph all my moves on the stage—the dance moves—I do it all, man. I program the drum machines, I beatbox like nobody can ever beatbox before. And I challenge anybody in rapping, beatboxing, and dancing. You know, it's just that's how I grew up. I was a battleaxe; I battled other people doing it. I'd go home in front of a mirror by myself and learn, and go back out on the streets and battle people in front of crowds.

BK: Was there one time when you just actually realized what was going on?

ICE: Oh, yeah. No doubt about that. Push record. This is a good one. That was a good question right there.

> Finally!

ICE: When I first found out—see, I've been on tour. I don't get to watch TV, MTV. I didn't know how big it actually had gotten so quick because I don't get to watch TV. Like I say, go from town to town. When I'm in the bus, I sleep And when I'm awake, I'm doing a concert, you know. And it's just like that; you don't get to hear radio. I don't hear nothing. I get to read newspapers and stuff with whatever they send me. And stuff they send me is usually months behind. So it's like, you know, it's not as big as it's gotten in the next month. John and I went to—John is my road manager—I go, man, I'm gonna go shopping. And it's like, no big deal. I'm gonna go shopping like normal before, you know. And I went to this mall in Minneapolis. And man, I walked in there like I was just gonna shop like it's nothing, you know. Soon as I walked—before I even got in the door—people outside noticed me, were just staring at me.

I was like, man, what's up? Do I have some food on my tooth or something? My fly undone? What's happening, you know? And I walk in and one little girl says, 'Oh, my God, it's Vanilla Ice,' you know, and just starts tripping out and everybody—there must have been 450 people all of a sudden. I had to hire the whole mall's security, which consisted of seven security guards. It was outrageous. And right then and there I go, oh my God. It's gotten huge.

I got to experience the mall with Ice, it's a good story, "push record." After our interview, Vanilla Ice and I ventured to the Beverly Center, a renowned upscale mall in Los Angeles. He aimed to acquire some "ice"—slang for jewelry. Upon entering the store, his presence was quickly recognized, and within moments, a crowd of about a hundred people gathered outside. Unlike his previous experience in Minneapolis, where mall security intervened, this time it was just his road manager John, his bodyguard Chill, the pop star himself, and me. Suddenly thrust into the role of an impromptu bodyguard, I assisted in forming a protective circle to escort him safely back to the hotel. Amusingly, I found myself declining autograph requests on his behalf, asserting, "Ice isn't doing autographs," a decision I made independently. I am a natural.

Throughout the 1990s, I had the opportunity to interview Ice several more times. He consistently supported my events, often promoting his appearances on various reality TV shows. Despite the fluctuations in his career, he maintained a positive attitude, even when those around him did not. He was my first cover story. You always remember your first...

> MY FIRST CHECK FOR WRITING THE VANILLA ICE COVER STORY. "STOP, COLLABORATE, AND...CASH IT!"

"WHEN YOU GOT ALL THE TIME IN THE WORLD, YOU WISH YOU HAD ALL THE MONEY IN THE WORLD. WHEN YOU GOT ALL THE MONEY IN THE WORLD, YOU WISH YOU HAD ALL THE TIME IN THE WORLD."

Vanilla Ice

BACKSTAGE HARMONY: NATE, WANYA, SHAWN, AND ME—STILL MAKING MEMORIES WITH BOYZ II MEN IN VEGAS, 2017.

I'VE BEEN FORTUNATE TO INTERVIEW MANY ARTISTS AT THE VERY BEGINNING OF THEIR CAREERS— way before inflated egos, platinum records, mansions, private jets, sold out world tours and Las Vegas residencies. With Boyz II Men, I was excited to sit down with them for their debut album CooleyHighHarmony, as their single "MotownPhilly" was already popping in heavy rotation on radio, with a second single "So Hard to Say Goodbye to Yesterday" climbing the charts as well. Hit records always break the ice in an interview. I remember prepping and thinking that while I loved the energy of their first single, their ballads shined the brightest, showcasing their vocals and harmonies. No shit…

I wasn't reviewing the record, just promoting it and getting to know the group. Well, at least half of the group as Wanyá Morris and Michael McCary were back at the studio working on the remix to their third single, "Uhh Ahh," not my favorite-I think the Boyz would second that emotion. So it was up to Nathan Morris and Shawn Stockman to win me over, kidding of course.

One of the main outlets I was doing this interview for was the "Fly Jock" radio legend Tom Joyner and his syndicated radio show On The Move which meant I had to bring some funny to the mix. And due to the magic of radio, the idea was for me to interview on behalf of Tom Joyner, so I had the guys address me as Tom (as my voice would be edited out). Thankfully, I went on to interview them several more times as the albums and hits kept coming but you always remember your first, and this was our first classic conversation.

NATHAN MORRIS (N): Nice microphone there, that's dope I like that.

BK: Watch this. Ah man check this out.

> This is where I do my extended microphone trick. Here's the visual, picture a thin wand with a mini microphone on the end. And then, I speak softly and sweetly, and like magic, the wand starts to grow.

SHAWN STOCKMAN (S): That's fly.

N: Oh, an extension. Bob Barker microphone.

S: Whoa. Yeah, yeah, right one of them things
[hums *The Price is Right* theme]

BK: We have spokesmodels out there in the back, don't worry.

> We are off to a great start, just like I like it. Time for voice distinctions so when we listen back in the studio, we know who was saying what.

N: This is Nathan Alex Vanderpool Morris from Boyz II Men. You know, the four guys that sing those songs? That's me, how you doing?

S: And what's up, this is Shawn Slim Stockman.

BK: Hey Slim. Why do they call you Slim? You looking like you gained, I think you gained weight since the video, no?

S: I gained a pound. I'm 141 pounds now. [laughs]

N: That was that candy bar last week. [laughs]

BK: Gotta watch what you eat man. Ay, wait what group are you guys a part of?

S: We're a part of Boyz II Men, I think, yeah.

N: I think it's boys, is it Boyz II Men? Boyz II Men yeah.

BK: Okay so you're half of, you're 50% of Boyz II Men, is that right?

S: That's right, one half of Boyz II Men here.

BK: Now if you had to describe this half as opposed to the other half, what would we talk about here?

S: Wanyá "Squirt" Morris and Michael "Bass" McCary. They're in the studio right now, working on our third single. Remix, "Uhh Ahh."

BK: [Singing the song] Uhh ahh

S: Yeah, yeah. That's right.

> They both laughed at my singing, so I came back at them with my own zinger.

BK: So how did you come up with that title? [Nate groans]

S: A lot of thought, took a lot of thought. A lot of brain juice, you know.

N: The spelling was like the hardest.

BK: But on the serious, I mean that's actually really, that's a good song, I mean.

> Okay, I may have fibbed on this one a little. But it's at the beginning of the interview, so no use insulting the subjects or their art. Besides, no one got hurt.

S: Thank you.

N: Thanks, man. Appreciate it.

BK: What's the story behind that song?

N: Well, what happened was we was at my house in Philly one time. And Michael, called us on the phone and said, "we need to write a song for the ladies," you know, "some song that has like, some kind of moaning and different things like that." He said, "we should write a song called 'Uhh Ahh.'"

S: Yep.

N: And nobody wanted to write it.

S: That's right.

> And no one should have. Okay...now I went too far. I'm actually listening to the song as I write, and I think I like it better now. I still don't care for the music video, but I digress.

N: So, you know, we [laughs] we flipped the coin. And unfortunately, Wanyá was the one that had to write the song. So, he went and started the song. And then after he finished, you know, he brought it to me, and I changed a lot of the words around and then we added a spice to it and made it what it is.

BK: Now explain, you say "added the spice" because there is definitely some sort of a spice to a Boyz II Men song. There's a connection throughout, so even though you got a fast, you got a slow, just the connection. Is there, I mean, am I saying that off top my head or do you agree with that?

S: Well, the way I guess the way we arranged the songs on the album, I guess it sort of like connects. I mean, like, each song seems like it goes together. I mean, after you hear "MotownPhilly," you automatically, like feel that "Under Pressure" is about to come on next, and so on and so forth. So, I guess the way we arranged the album makes it feel like a whole connection, which is good.

N: We tried to put it in the order that if you listen to the tape, say like if you listen to the tape and all of a sudden your phone rang and you picked it up, the tape would be off—it was like, you know, it would just go off and you wouldn't even notice that the songs have ended. So, it would be like a continuous flow to like, it wouldn't seem like you'd be sitting there for about 10 to 20 minutes, it seemed like five minutes.

BK: Yeah, now let's start with what was actually the first question I was gonna ask. What's going on with you guys now? You know, as far as it's like, you must be still in the middle of that success. You know, it's gotta be hitting you right now.

N: Well, it is, we still not really feeling it yet, though. I mean, you know, we go to shows, you know, crazy crowd, 25,000 to 30,000 people. But I don't know, I really don't feel it yet. I just, I don't even feel it's a job. I just feel we just go out and sing. And that's it.

S: It's just a whole lot of fun. That's all, just doing what we've dreamed of doing. Yeah, it's just a lot of fun. We're just enjoying ourselves having the times of our lives.

BK: You dream about this. Is it everything you expected? You know, when you're sitting there and you're like, "I'm gonna have an album someday" and you have it. Is it everything you expected?

S: No. This, yes, it's a little bit more. We didn't expect as much hard work, it's a lot of hard work that you got to put into performing and recording albums and things like that. But don't get me wrong, it's fun, you know what I mean? And we wouldn't trade it for the world. But, you know, it's a lot of hard work. A lot of those people who think that, you know, singing and dancing is glamor and glitz. It's not. It takes a lot of hard work and a lot of dedication, you know, to become successful.

BK: "MotownPhilly" was a song that basically when I heard, I mean I do this for a living—I knew there's something special about it, right away. What about you guys, did you know this was gonna launch you like it had?

S&N: No.

N: We didn't [they both laugh]. Actually, we didn't even want to release that as a single, we wanted to drop a ballad. But the president of Motown [Records] Jheryl Busby saying we should do this one because, you know, it's a good introduction to the group and, and it says like Boyz II Men, like six zillion times throughout the song: "Boyz II Men, Boyz II Men, Boyz II Men, Boyz II Men." So, he says this is the one, great introduction song. So, we went with him and put it out. And luckily, we did.

BK: So basically, if someone hears that song, and they don't know what group you're in, it's kind of..

S: Yeah, they should pretty much know.

N: We get questions sometimes. I mean, we have a song called "MotownPhilly." And people still ask us where we from.

BK: Hey where you guys from?

S: Kansas City, [laughs] nah from Philadelphia.

BK: You are from Philly!

S&N: Yeah.

s: Oh yeah. n: We're from Philly. 'MotownPhilly,' Philly.

bk: Oh, I get it

n: *Some people even think there's a town called MotownPhilly. Some people say, "Where you from? MotownPhilly?" No, just Philly.*

s: That's funny, I didn't know that. n: "Swear that you guys live in MotownPhilly."

bk: MotownPhilly is between Philly and Detroit.

s: Yeah. n: [laughs] It's somewhere in there right. s: A new town.

> This was a mix of great answers and comedy, my two favorite things in an interview.

bk: Okay but on the same token, when "MotownPhilly" did hit, like it HIT, you know? People, you know, if they pick up the album, throw it on, it's like all these ballad tunes. Like you're dropping ballads.

n: Yeah, that's what we wanted to do. We felt that that was a strong point. So we just wanted to come out with that first, but they deterred us and put out "MotownPhilly." And we're not complaining, sold over a million records. So, we're very happy, very happy.

bk: So we're talking like ballads. You said the strong suit. I mean, you know, Shawn, you agree or?

s: Oh, yeah, definitely. We thought that, you know, since dropping the ballad, you know, first would display our vocal talents a lot better because we do a lot of singing and you could hear our singing abilities a lot better on ballads. Because up-tempos, you don't really have a chance to you know, display a talent because it's so fast. But Jheryl made the call about doing "MotownPhilly" and he was right. Thanks Jheryl.

BK: Say, "Hey, Mr. Busby, I think you're wrong right now."

S: Hey, man, he's really been you know, he's another person who really helped us out. He's like a father to us. He really takes care of us.

BK: Well so now you dropped the ballad. And look what happened.

N: Yeah, so I guess we both were right. We just had the timing off. And we well, we honestly—we didn't even want to drop this one next.

BK: Why don't you want to? It's such a nice song ("It's So Hard To Say Goodbye To Yesterday")

N: Well, actually, what happened was, and Jheryl felt this too. He said that an acapella song, he didn't think would be a big radio hit. So, we were thinking about dropping, "Please Don't Go." But radio forced us to drop it. So, thank you radio.

BK: Someone started playing it and?

N: And then people just start picking up on it. And thanks to them, we've sold 500,000 copies of that one.

BK: All right.

S: We went gold. So, we'd like to thank all those supporters and buyers, consumers.

> Radio has been a dying medium ever since I first got into the game. But one thing it does do is "break" songs, which means "makes them hits." Most times the record label creatives pick the singles that become the hits, but every once in a while there are happy accidents that go "Gold." I think in this particular case, this song showcased their vocal talents which is something the guys wanted to get across in their debut. Not to mention the sentiment of the song. Cue the obvious question.

BK: Now as far as the song goes, what is the song saying? "It's So Hard to Say Goodbye to Yesterday."

S: Well, I guess in general, the concept of the song is just a tune where if you miss someone, or someone is really deep into your thoughts, and you want to be with that special person—and you can't for some reason—you're just thinking about those good times that you had with that person. I mean, *"It's Hard to Say Goodbye to Yesterday"* is one of those songs that helps you do that. You know what I mean?

BK: I don't remember who said it, but you wanted to show off your vocals. That's got to be one of the strongest points to your group. What goes on vocally with you guys?

S: Oh, definitely. It is a strong point. It is the very strongest point of Boyz II Men. I mean, Boyz II Men's concept is just based around our vocals and how we sing and everything. So yeah, vocals are very important for us.

BK: Who arranges the vocals? How does it work? The creative process behind the band?

N: Sometimes it's all of us. And sometimes it depends on who writes the song, somebody might write a song and bring it to the group already arranged, or somebody might write half of it, and then bring it to another group member and they finish the other half or something like that. But it's like a combination of everybody most of the time.

BK: As far as even the vocals like who sings? What? When? Who does lead? Who does, you know…

N: Well, we try to make sure everybody sings on every song. We just put, you know, if you sing the top, you take the top part. If you sing the bottom, you singing the bottom. The middle, the middle, just like that.

BK: I mean, I know a little bit about music. And it's like you say, it's like so easy, but people out there, they don't realize. They're like "hey, how did they do that?"

S: Yeah, it's a lot of hard work that goes into it. I mean we get into little conflicts once in a while, as far as what we think should be in a certain part. But eventually it starts to gel and we make it, you know, comes out, and everything.

BK: So, as far as creative process goes, everybody has a hand in this. Anything specific that you want to get on your debut album, like, "you know what, we want to do a song about this," or "we got to highlight this."

N: Well, we didn't even, you know, look at it that way. We wrote songs. We had songs together before we even became a group. I mean, majority of the songs on the album, you know, people had wrote before they even met each other.

BK: I didn't know that.

N: Well actually, "Please Don't Go" is like the oldest song on the album. It's about seven years old, so.

BK: Shit, you wrote it when you were like 12?

N: I wrote it in ninth grade. And this was before the group even got together. So, it's like, we don't sit down and say, "well, we're going to write this song for this person," or "we're going to write this song for this image or R&B or pop." We just write and, you know, we hope that everybody can like what we write.

BK: We have another interview with Mike (Michael Bivins of New Edition & Bell Biv DeVoe), you know, you're talking a lot about Michael. And, are you guys sick of that already?

S: Oh no, no, it's cool. We expect that. Because I mean, Michael is a public figure. And, he did help us, and he plays a major part in our career, so.

N: There's only one question that's always asked when we're doing promotional stuff. And when we're about to go on stage and a fan might say, "where's Michael at?" Like, we just supposed to know where he is all the time.

BK: Hey where's Michael at right now? (I had to)

N: Well, I do know this time he's in LA right now.

> Their discovery story is of legend, singing "Can You Stand The Rain" by New Edition to members of New Edition backstage at a New Edition concert. Say that ten times fast.

BK: What goes through your mind when you hear that song?

N: The backstage audition for Michael.

BK: You still remember that, like as clear as day?

N: Yep. S: Mhm.

BK: What were you wearing? What was going on?

N: Black turtlenecks and there was a lot of different people back there. I mean, when we sang for him, we sang for basically more than just him. I mean, Ricky [Bell] and Ronnie DeVoe were back there, Cherrelle was there, Keith Sweat was back there. Paula Abdul was back there. Patti LaBelle. There was a lot of people there.

S: And the thing about it, I don't know about the other guys, but I wasn't nervous.

N: Of course not.

S: I mean, it was like our one shot you know, to sing so we were like, "hey, the heck with it." You know what I mean?

N: And we weren't even like trying to do it actually for a record deal. We just wanted somebody to you know, just to hear what we sound like. And I'm not complaining.

BK: Did you know you nailed it? Did you nail it? Or did you guys think you could have done better?

S: Well, we felt good about it. I mean, when we did it, we kind of knew that it sounded good. But as far as him accepting it, Michael Bivins. I mean, we didn't know what to expect with him. But I mean, we did it. And we kind of were confident about how it sounded and everything.

BK: Now you kind of know him as a person, what's he like? People out there want to know what Mike Bivins is like?

S: Real cool, down to earth, very funny at times. He has

you laughing with this personality. He's a very cool cool brother. He's very nice. He's our pal. He's our brother at times. And sometimes he plays a father figure or two.

N: Sometimes he's, yeah.

BK: "Yeaaah."

N: Right. Sometimes he's just right. Yeah. BK & S: Yeah.

N: Yeah S: Yeah. N: And that's Michael. S: Yeah, that's Mike.

> Okay I kept this Laurel and Hardy comedy routine in this transcript for a reason, hopefully the back and forth is as funny on the page as it was in the conference room at 6255 Sunset Boulevard. But the real reason I kept it in is that over 30 years later when I think of Boyz II Men, I don't even think about Michael Bivins' association with the group. I don't think anyone does, and I'm pretty sure that before they hit the stage now, no one asks "Where's Mike?"

BK: Alright now here's a question you haven't heard before (dripping with sarcasm). So, how'd you guys meet? I just wanted to get some background bio, you know, bio information?

S: That is a different question. N: Yeah, never heard that before.

BK: Probably never heard that one huh.

> Again, this isn't Shakespeare, David Frost, or Dan Rather asking questions...but at least I ask with some version of humor which keeps it fresh.

s: Well, how did we meet? How did we meet?

n: We all attended the High School of Performing Arts in Philadelphia. Well actually, me and Michael met in '85. Because me and Michael were in the same year. And then Shawn came in, in '86, and Wanyá came into the school in '87. But we didn't actually become a group until, like '89. We all in the same choir and you know, we used to sing a lot, rehearse our music for choir and then we would sing some other songs on the side.

BK: Did you guys click right away?

n: Well, it took a little while. I mean, the sound was there. Just took the personalities a little while to get together as far as everybody clicking.

s: We were group members before we were like, really friends.

> I'm going to skip the neighborhood talk, the buying your mom stuff and go straight to a theory that I've witnessed many times in practice: Fame and fortune is one hell of an aphrodisiac.

BK: Do women start to treat you a little differently now?

s: A little bit.

n: No. Yes, they do. There's no "little bit" about it. Yes, they do.

BK: Talk to me, like what goes on now?

n: Yeah, it's kind of awkward. I mean, we just always as a group, we always sit down and we have the slogan that "if it wasn't for Boyz II Men, we know we wouldn't be getting all this attention from a lot of females that we do." But I mean, we try to take it in stride and just you know, adjust to it. It's kind of silly in a way though, that people act the way they do, you know? They didn't want to be down, but now they want to be down, you know? We just take it in one day at a time.

s: Way of life.

BK: What does your family, your friends think about what's been happening and do they support you? Lots people say, "I'm going into music." People give the old, "Uhh…"

N: They thought it was a joke from the beginning. But you know, I think it took for them to hear it on the radio to actually be convinced.

BK: What about for you?

N: For me? I was into it from day one, wholeheartedly from the beginning. I kind of just thought it had to work.

BK: You had to.

N: Yep.

BK: You ever think about giving up or anything?

N: Nope.

BK: Well, what was it about that? You just said, "Hey, man, I'm holding on. I'm keeping this up. I got this dream?"

N: I just, I don't know, man. I just felt that this was right. That's all.

s: He speaks for all of us. He speaks for all of us.

BK: He just says it.

s: Says it all, said it all.

BK: Did you even think about doing something else?

s: Uh no. At least, well we were, I was planning on going to college. But I mean, I really had to give this a try first because I wouldn't feel like—I had to feel like you know, I had to do this first before I did anything else just to satisfy me. And I'm kind of glad that I did.

> Having zero plan B is a continuous theme in entertainment success. Born to do it, whatever you want to call it. I've interviewed countless artists that felt the same way, but 90% of them never get over that hump. They might get that first record deal or movie contract, maybe even have some modicum of success but to be able to build, maintain, and continue doing what they love can be harder than the initial break. These boys have succeeded beyond.

BK: Okay, second to last question. As far as the touring goes, when people come see the Boyz II Men show, what to expect? What do you think you're going to see?

N: You should expect a lot of singing. s: Mhm.

N: A lot. We definitely make singing our strong point, because a lot of people just get on stage and let the band go through the music and have their background singers sing everything. And they sing little parts and speak most of the lyrics. But you will see, hear a lot of singing from Boyz II Men.

BK: As far as getting in front of people, you guys nervous? You mentioned you weren't nervous back then. I guess some people like the recording process, some people like this, some people love getting in front of and performing.

N: The only show I was ever nervous on was the

first show we did after our record came out. And after that it's been a piece of cake ever since.

s: Yeah.

> So here's where I have to insert one of my favorite industry stories as it deals with a Boyz II Men show in 2017, during one of their Las Vegas residencies at the Mirage Hotel. I had reached out to Nate to let him know I'd be in town, and would love to bring my queen to the show. Nate texted me instructions on how to pick up the tickets ('I will have someone meet you at a nondescript door by the box office'), and invited us for a meet and greet prior to the show. Turns out, we were the "meet and greet" as it was just us in their dressing room right before the show. There was a moment of wow, I cannot believe 26 years later I am sitting backstage with these guys who have a sold out show that night. By the way, there were no nerves happening pre-show, it seemed like a "piece of cake." All I remember is saying to them that I think we should leave, as in "don't you have to go on the stage?" Well, we did leave and they did go on stage minutes later. I wish I was reviewing the show as I would have lit them up, deservingly so. Here's why, they have hits and they delivered. But they truly connected with the audience as seasoned professionals do. They even had a moment during their performance of "I'll Make Love To You," Nate, Shawn, and Wanyá literally go into the audience stocked with roses and allow fans (mostly ladies with the blessings of their partners) to come get a kiss, a selfie, and a rose. Talk about a concert memory, I wish Jheryl Busby was alive to see his Boyz hold court.

BK: Now as far as the future for you guys, as far as thinking about the next album, do you know what road, where you want to take it, which way you want to go?

N: We're gonna just cross that bridge when we come to it. We're just gonna ride this out, have fun with this one.

Okay, so I'm not taking full credit, but my last question was "what road" did you want to take and less than a year later, they released their massive hit song "End of The Road" which peaked atop the charts and set a then-record spending 13 weeks at number one. Coincidence?

The Boyz later broke this record twice more with the singles "I'll Make Love to You" and "One Sweet Day" (with Mariah Carey) which, at 14 and 16 weeks respectively, set records for the most weeks at number one at the time. When "On Bended Knee" took the number one spot away from "I'll Make Love to You," Boyz II Men became the third musical act, after The Beatles and Elvis Presley, to replace themselves atop the Billboard Hot 100.

But those are just stats that you can google, ask Siri or the latest artificial intelligence application. But, here's some real talk and real takeaways.

These kids were working on their craft and ready to go, and when the opportunity presented itself, they delivered. And they kept delivering. I am beyond happy for them, and they have been good to me throughout my career, showing up to my events countless times. It's not about me, it's about them realizing that even though they "made it" in this business, they still put in the work which is why these boys have become men, and this conversation is a classic.

NATE MORRIS MICHAEL S. McCARY

Boyz II Men

SHAWN STOCKMAN   WANYA MORRIS

Boyz II Men's first publicity photo— signed, sealed, but not personalized.

TLC's Legacy: dozens of girl trios including Premiere and Drama, proving I wasn't just chasing waterfalls—I was delivering the *'funniest and funnest'* interviews in the game.

I'M GONNA BE HONEST, when I first interviewed TLC for their debut album, I had ZERO idea they would become one of the best selling female groups of all time—groups, not R&B groups, but groups. I think The Spice Girls reign supreme, and The Supremes are still the American champions, but wowza. I mean, I thought En Vogue would be "bigger" which goes to show I didn't have my pulse on the female music scene or psyche. I still don't, but I digress.

Keep in mind, I'm talking to TLC in 1992 and I remember them clearly, how could you not? For starters, they're wearing crazy colorful outfits and condoms. Yes, condoms, ALL types of condoms safety-pinned onto their clothes. Prophylactics as a fashion statement? At the time, I was thinking "gimmick." The reality was that they were talking about sex and sexuality in a very open way, not necessarily promoting but rather normalizing. They know kids are hooking up, so why not make "protection" cool, especially since it was only a few months earlier that Magic Johnson shocked the world when he announced he was HIV positive.

These were serious times, yet not in this conference room at Arista Records. T-Boz, Left Eye, and Chilli together were loud, lively, having fun and ready to publicize. If you saw any of their old interviews, they kick into promo mode pretty quickly, singing and rapping together to anyone who would listen. If you're not old enough to remember the ups and downs of their career—the bankruptcies and breakups, the famous boyfriends, the fire-setting of a house—you can watch their documentary *TLC Forever* to find out about their storied career. And of course, there was the tragic loss of Lisa "Left Eye" Lopes in a car accident in 2002. There are many reasons to include TLC in this book.

That's not why they're a classic conversation. I'm including the trio because of the **FUN** I had with them, and the **FUN** they had with me. All I did was press record on the tape machine. We didn't even have a mic check for proper levels, they began loud and got louder and I loved it.

BK: Test test test. Hey, okay, how does that sound?

CHILLI(C): [putting on a low sexy voice] Hi, and who are you? I'm Chilli, I mean I know it sounds like I have a hormonal problem, but I'm really okay. [back in her real voice] Okay, I'm Chilli.

LEFT EYE(LE): Left Eye.

T-BOZ(TB): Yo I'm T-Boz.

BK: How's that go again?

[TLC rapping]

TB: I'm the t-tiggeda-tiggeda-T-Boz.

LE: I'm the liggy-liggy-Left Eye.

C: And I bring the chill-Chilli.

TLC: And that is Ooooh…on the TLC tip!

BK: All right there you go, debut record. Is it everything you expected that a debut record would be like?

LE: No, no, no. Well, let's see what did I expect? Actually,

I didn't know what exactly to expect. I mean, I expected popularity, I expected.... amongst other things, no, I don't know if a lot of things took me by surprise because things that I didn't think would happen really happened for real.

BK: Like?

C: Countdown. LE: Countdown. Yes, hearing my song on the countdown, seeing my picture on a tape cassette, on a CD...

TB: Radio too.

BK: Alright, c'mon keep going.

TB: Hearing it on the radio period, I was just adding on to her little comment.

BK: We like adding.

C: Our very own video instead of being on someone else's video, our video, so.

BK: What was that feeling when you heard yourself on the radio, T-Boz?

TB: [laughing] That is a feeling, well Left Eye and I experienced it at the same time. Chilli couldn't be there with us at the same time.

C: [mock whine]

TB: Poor thing, yeah poor baby, booger. But it was the most. [sighs]

C: Tell him what y'all did, what's up, go to Left Eye.

LE: We pulled in Taco Bell and got out the car and started dancing.

BK: Dancing with your burritos?

LE: No, we didn't get them yet. We were just dancing.

BK: Okay, just making sure.

TB: We turned red in the face. It was like we just lost our brother like [mimics gasping for air] "Ain't 2 Proud 2 Beg!" Started dancing.

LE: What made it so good was one of our favorite artists was just on, Naughty by Nature. We were complimenting them and saying, "Man when we come on the radio like, that's gonna be so fly!" Next thing you know, break, bash, go, smash, "Ain't 2 Proud 2 Beg!" Now, pull right in the thing, and got out the car, started dancing.

BK: What do you know? Boy, Taco Bell, an institution.

TLC: Yeah.

BK: Yeah! Alright now, when we introduce you everybody has names here you know like T-Boz for instance. Where did you get that name? What does it stand for? How did it come about?

TB: All right now. The T stands for Tionne, that's my real name. Boz is slang for boss. It means Tionne is the boss, I'm the boss, but you call me Boz. T-Boz

BK: As in T Boss. Now, boy it's getting chilly in here. Talk to me Chilli.

C: Well, how'd I get my name? Because T-Boz and Left Eye are not complete without chili sauce. I add all the hot sauce to the group and then it's complete. So that's how I get my name.

BK: Ah, want to say what your real name is or keep it private?

C: My real name's Rozonda, but don't you think I look more like a chilli?

BK: You looking so chilly, whoa frigid. Chilly, that's not the chili you are. It's not red hot chili with like beans and stuff?

C: Oh no, not no nothing to give you gas or anything, no of course not [laughter in the room].

BK: No, that's up to Left Eye…

LE: Yeah, right

[more room laughter]

BK: Okay

LE: Left Eye, my name's Left Eye because the eye is right, thank you!

BK: What?

LE: Because the eye is right, thank you!

> Okay, I still don't know what that means. But, I wasn't going to ask a third time.

BK: Just making sure, we got to get these things out of the way. Okay, you guys are very, you know, very down and very morbid. You know, just no life to you at all. No personality or anything. Is this true?

> This is BK sarcasm in the house. What you can't tell from a transcript is the emotion, the loudness, the laughter. It was all there. It's as if they all just had triple macchiatos and Red Bulls. Their energy goes to eleven.

C: We just have no way to go, I mean, it's just

like, who understands? [everyone laughs] I mean, really? What? What do you think?

BK: [in a monotone voice] Well, let me tell you Chill-

C: Could we please have some eye contact here? [the girls laughs] I mean, I'm looking dead at you and you're looking the other way. I mean, is it something that I said or something?

> Chilli understands the BK sarcasm, and hits back with some TLC sarcasm.

BK: What do you think Left Eye?

TB: Yeah, what's going on babe?

LE: Well, you know, what was the question?

C: Yeah, what was the question?

> Hilarious!!! Just ask me...

BK: T-Boz, let me ask you a question. What do you think about the partner to your left? If you had to describe booger [TLC laughter], I mean Chilli [more laughter]. First talk about musically, what does she bring to TLC? And then personally, what is Chilli like?

TB: Musically, she's R&B. We have funk, R&B, and rap. And Chilli's the R&B singer of the group. Personally, she has a lot of energy and she's outgoing, she's fun. She coordinates a lot of things, group-wise as far as dancers. And that's all. I don't like her for real, I just pretend [giggles], nah I'm just joking. Other than that, she's a little hot mama, sexy mama of the group. She has the sauce.

BK: She has that sauce. Alright now Chilli, if you can describe yourself. No actually, if you can look to your left, talk about Left Eye. What does Left Eye bring to the group both musically, then personally?

C: Okay, musically? Well Left Eye is like the Flavor Flav of the group you know, it's like…

BK: I don't see a watch [laughter in the room]. But anyway…

C: Left Eye, I mean, you look at her and just think that okay, well, she's a kid, what can she do? I mean, she can rap her butt off. And it's like, she's not like any other rapper. She has her own style. That's why she is a part of TLC because everybody is original. You know, no one is like anybody else. She got it going on. You know what I'm saying yo.

BK: Personally, what's she like?

C: Left Eye is, she's a lot of fun. She's very energetic. You know, sometimes we just wish she just go away because…no, I'm just playing. She farts all the time. Left Eye is real open, very open, she don't care. I mean, she cares but she doesn't. If it's something natural, if you have to do it, she'll do it with no problems and say, "Hey, what's up? How you are doing?" You know, but Left Eye is a great person.

BK: What's up, how you doing?

LE: How you doing? [makes a farting sound]. Oops, excuse me.

BK: That's okay. Feel free, feel open.

c: It's a natural thing.

LE: It's in our nature.

BK: Alright, now if you could do me a favor, see T-Boz over there? Let's talk musically about T-Boz, and then personally, what's she like?

LE: If TLC was FLC, her name would be funkiness. T-Boz brings the funk to the group for real for real. And I think that a lot of our songs sound as good as they do because of her funk. No regular singer could have seen what she's singing and, you know, made the song, gave it that extra little flavor or specialness about it. But T-Boz, she's cool. She's the boss. She's laid back, hard looking, softie on the inside. She's a very rational person, she keeps us out of trouble you know. And she's very levelheaded, smart and everything like that, fun to be with.

BK: Alright we got the idea. What am I like?

c: You know what? If you were a girl, we'd have you in the Wench Mob.

BK: What does it take to be a member of the Wench Mob?

c: Well, I say if you are female, are you a female?

BK: What else?

c: And you have to be down with TLC, y'know what I'm saying?

> I'm 100% down with TLC, but I didn't make it into the Wench Mob because of obvious reasons. Although, if I identified as a female back then, I would be the leader of the Wench Mob!

BK: Name of the album for those listeners out there who want to pick it up, it's?

TLC: "Oooooh… On the TLC Tip" [singing together].

BK: You have your record, what do you think about it? It's your first try. Talk about it, feel free to be biased.

C: I love our album. I mean, I think it's great. It's like, I can listen to it and not skip over one song and say, "Well, I like this song better than that." You know, saying I like all of our songs. And I think that when people buy our album, please do (she's good), you know they'll be able to relate to at least one song. How many songs we have? 11? I'm sure more than that. We love, I love the album. I'm excited about it. And it still hits me every now and then, I can't believe it.

BK: Yeah, I'll pinch you, there you go.

C: You don't pinch me hard enough.

> It may seem creepy in print, but it was all good fun, laughter filled the room.

BK: T-Boz what are your feelings on the record?

TB: I feel fortunate and blessed to have such a good album. These days some people might talk about anything, but our album's really based on real life situations. And then we stand for something at the same time. But I can't believe when I listen to it like, "Gosh, that's me." I mean, you know, I'm saying like my dreams have come true.

> A sweet takeaway here. She's saying and we're hearing genuine excitement of dreams coming true in real time. What's crazy, sexy, and cool about that is I'm sure she had to keep coming up with new dreams as the hits and success kept coming.

BK: Left Eye, what are your feelings?

LE: About this album? Okay, I feel so fortunate to have, you know, been able to work with such producers as L.A. (Reid), Babyface, Marley Marl, Dallas Austin, Jermaine Dupri, we've worked with the top people, you couldn't get any better. And that in itself is unbelievable. Because these are people who I have admired before I, you know, met them and they just seem so untouchable. But when you have the chance, I mean, that's a once in a lifetime chance that a lot of people dream about, and everyone does not have that chance. So, I'm very fortunate. I'll never forget it. And when our second and our third and fourth album comes around, we will be going back to the same people.

BK: Now the music side of it is very upbeat and funky from a woman's perspective in a sense. Can you talk about that aspect? Obviously, you're women…

LE: Yeah, we're women. Of course. No, but we think the other women need a female role model.

There are female role models out there but there are none like us you know. We represent freedom, independence, being what you want to be—

BK: Fight the power!

> TLC laughs, they were a good audience for my stand-up interviewing routine.

BK: Ah yeah, you know, I'm sure you've been asked many times about your glasses, your hair pieces, your clothing and yes, you guys wear…

TLC: Condoms!

LE: Okay, yes, we're the condom ladies now. But we knew before we put these condoms on it might, you know, be controversial. And it is controversial. We've gotten a lot of feedback from it. Sometimes positive, sometimes negative, you know, there's people out there who like us because we can sit up here and tell people to be safe when it comes to having sex because it is happening, it's reality. But then there are some people who sitting there talking about, "You can't do that. You cannot wear condoms." But you know, hey, we never asked everyone to like what we're doing and we're not pushing our ideas on anyone. We're making what we believe in available to those who want to listen.

BK: To me when I was growing up, I was taught that only the male can wear a condom.

LE: Which is true, but only a male can wear a condom, but a female can buy one and bring it to the table.

TB: Or the date. Because a lot of people will, they'll have sex without having a condom because they're ashamed to go buy one. And if you're going to have sex, you must have safe sex. So if TLC is weird, if TLC wears condoms and they say, "Oh, might look like a fashion statement and make it fun at the same time."

LE: There's like a million ways you can present a condom. And we tried to do it the clean way you know. We wear very baggy, colorful, playful… We wear other things hanging off our clothes, condoms just one of 'em. But everything we do wear represents something.

C: And it's not like we're taking them out of the package and let them hang out, looking all nasty and stuff.

TB: *We're not saying, "go and have sex." We're saying since you are having sex be safe and protection is priority.*

BK: T-Boz can you stand up one more time? I want to see that condom, I've been looking for one that size.

TB: Oh really?

BK: Yeah.

TB: Will you marry me? [laughs] Big condom.

BK: Big condoms!

> I know I alluded in my intro that TLC brought awareness to safe sex, made it normal. And I just mentioned in the interview, that usually it's the guy who is responsible for buying, having a condom. My have times changed, and I say that because back then, that WAS the reality. Women didn't go on dates with a condom in their purse, and they didn't have them in their nightstand. In fact, if they did, they would be considered a little "loose, somewhat slutty." But today, there's no negative connotation if a woman is carrying, it's almost equally expected. Not saying that TLC is responsible for this social sea change, but they were definitely ahead of their time.

BK: Anyhow so I guess I should move, so let me go down to the creative process, how did you guys pick songs? Did you write any of the songs? Can you talk about that aspect?

TB: Mhm. C: No, we can't.

BK: Alright well, I wasn't talking to each of you, I know Left Eye can so…

LE: Hi, this is Left Eye. I write all of my raps so T-Boz and Chilli, they write also, they've written on the album. The concepts, but you know, the concepts in 90% of the case came from the producer. The producer would come to us with an idea and write about it and we would back it up. We were just there to vibe with them and add a little TLC touch.

BK: What brings that TLC tip or that flavor? What is the TLC? What makes it a TLC song, like when you guys started putting your voices on it? Chilli, I can tell you know the answer to that.

[Chilli laughs]

LE: No, no. Okay, now this is Left Eye now.

BK: How odd for Left Eye to talk!

LE: Now what makes this TLC without the voices like—well—it is really because no one is out there like T-Boz. And I know there are women, female artists who have sung in that type of voice but…

TB: It's mine.

LE: Now no, seriously, T-Boz, that's her thing. That's just her thing.

TB: We'll be trendsetters. Left Eye raps differently and Chilli sings it all together. It's a different package altogether.

BK: Well let me ask you about the fact, how did you end up getting a record deal? Like, how did you get discovered?

> Get ready for some TLC comedy…these girls are having fun and it shows even in a transcript.

C: We you know, we held up LaFace and we said, "look, you know, either record deal or we blow up the place." And you know, hey, look what happened—place is still there. And we have a record deal. I mean hey.

BK: Left Eye is that how it went?

LE: No. Not how it went, Chilli, Chilli always lies okay? What happened was, it was about 100 groups, and we went in a raffle.

C: She's not telling the truth either! Left Eye lies! Gotta talk to T-Boz this time. T-Boz you tell it better.

TB: The serious and real truth is, I am the serious person. I'm walking up the street and we see these contracts on the ground and pick them up and sign them.

LE: We like found somebody to take them to, you know. And we said okay [whispers sarcastically] we really had sex with everybody. No, we didn't.

BK: But safe sex.

TB: No seriously, we got a record contract through our manager Pebbles.

> Pebbles was a recording artist, yes I interviewed her. But her claim to fame in this particular story was that she was married to L.A. Reid, the "LA" in LaFace, the record label founded by him and his uber creative producing partner Babyface.

BK: You're with the LaFace family.

TB: I like LaFace regardless to who's signed to it really. I mean, they're the best record company for us I feel because we're kind of like a family. It's not like you have to call a record company and say, "well, can I speak to the person or the person to the person or the person?" I speak to you because we're close like that. That is one of the best record companies, we're fortunate and blessed to be signed to them really.

BK: That's a super songwriting production team. Can you talk about where these guys, I mean, they work with you. They're all over the record. What is it like working with these two guys?

LE: They're down to earth.

TB: Just like us...

LE: Yeah, they can be playful, they can be serious. They accept ideas freely with no problem at all. And we basically, we get along really well.

TB: I think it even makes it better being that they're so multi-talented, they're still down to earth. It even makes it, I mean just sparkle more.

BK: Now one of the things about your music is that you kind of want to dance. Can you describe since we can't envision you know, can you tell us you know what to expect, what's gonna happen?

LE: Okay, when you see a TLC show, you will see TLC moves and TLC steps…

TB: Created from TLC.

LE: Basically, you'll see new things and you'll probably have to watch the show about five times, catch on what we're doing. It's gonna be nice, you know.

BK: You digging the movement? You digging the dancing, digging that aspect? I mean, obviously, it's gotta come in.

LE: Well okay, I can say this about us. All of us are great dancers. We do a variety of dancing, we can all house. We can all freestyle. We can all do Atlanta style music, which is ghetto dancing, which is something totally different. Hip Hop, but now there's TLC—

TB: The ability to learn everything, can reset your mind so we can do it.

BK: TLC, what is TLC? You said now we can do TLC…

LE: TLC dances…

C: Dances, stuff we created ourselves. Nobody, nobody else doing these dances, just us.

> This is so true. Check out their *"Waterfalls"* video which came out two years after this conversation. Their TLC dance is totally unique, totally TLC.

BK: All right. Let me just get, and in the future-future, what would you like to see happen?

TB: Movies.

LE: Cartoons, sitcoms, commercials.

C: Everything.

I would have loved to see them do everything as these girls were so much fun, and talented to boot. At the time, I was just happy to have a fun interview, a conversation on a Friday afternoon heading into the weekend.

I didn't see TLC too much after this interview, several backstage media events and such, so I kind of lost track of their career. I didn't follow the pop culture tabloids, but I knew about the ups and downs reported in the press, so I always felt a little concerned for them as my memory was of three kids living their dreams in real time, beyond happy, fun-loving. I felt terrible when I heard the news of Lisa Lopes' death, still do. And I didn't know anything about T-Boz's health issues, but revisiting this interview put a huge smile on my face. These women are in the history books-their music, style and personas influenced this industry in the early '90s through today. Because of them, I had to interview dozens of female trios and quartets that never quite made an impact and are no longer around. TLC is…

R. Kelly's biggest influence? **Stevie Wonder.** Here's me with the genius himself, whose voice R. Kelly couldn't help but channel during our interview.

I DEBATED WITH MYSELF ABOUT INCLUDING R. KELLY IN THE BOOK, but honestly, he is literally one of my classic conversations in every sense of the term. He was new (so fresh and so clean), he was beyond talented, and you could tell that he would be a star. Insert many jokes here, but I am talking about my interview from 1992, way before the craziness.

I got the call to talk to him about his debut album with his group Public Announcement, but this was truly an R. Kelly album as he wrote, sang, and produced all the music including two number one R&B hits—"Honey Love" and "Slow Dance." The album *Born into the 90's* was not a masterpiece. In this case, you can literally judge a book by the album cover. Google it, I will wait—I'm kidding a little bit—but the music wasn't that new jack good.

I came in thinking this was just another interview not knowing if he was going to have a hit album or career, but I came out thinking I love this guy as a person, love his story, he says all the right things, seems genuine and he's really talented (and not because he sang to me a couple of times, although singing to me in an interview does get bonus points!). He was actually excited to be interviewed by me, and that alone classifies this as a classic conversation.

So when revisiting this interview, I reminded myself to think back to 1992 when Robert was just a new artist with a dream, way before becoming the most successful R&B artist of the '90s, before "I Believe I Can Fly" or countless trophies for Grammys, BET, Billboard, Soul Train, and NAACP Image Awards. I mean he won "Image" awards!!! Again, I'm thinking back to before the accusations of child abuse and child pornography, before the prosecutions and acquittals, before "Surviving R. Kelly" was a thing, before being sent back to prison. Hopefully you can try and do the same.

BK: So let's get that level. What should I call you?

R. KELLY: R. Kelly. Yes, that's cool.

BK: All right, just making sure. Hey, how you doing?

R. KELLY: All right. All right, man. Testing 123456.

BK: You used to this interview type of thing?

R. KELLY: Not really, just saying what I feel. You know?

BK: Is it difficult? It is nerve-racking.

R. KELLY: No because what I do man is real, you know, so I might as well just be real with it, you know? If it wasn't, then I would be doing the wrong thing I believe.

BK: We don't want you to do the wrong thing, especially on my interview.

R. KELLY: Why, right?

BK: Now, people want to hear about this. Because I mean, is it considered your debut? Do you consider this your debut record?

> Some context on why I'm asking this…he was with a previous group and had made some music, but the project was scrapped. You see, back then I was hip to this kind of stuff.

R. KELLY: Well, to be honest man, I never really understood what debut ever meant. You know, I just say it's my first album. Yeah, I hope that everybody gets into it because it's an album for everybody, you know, no matter what the color or whatever. It's just, it's a friend of yours. It's a friend of everybody's, my songs and my way of expressing music. It's just a friend of everybody's.

BK: Is it everything you expected your first album would be? When you said one day, I'm gonna have an album. Is it everything you expected? The dreams that you share? My album would be like…

R. KELLY: Well, this is everything I pray for, you know, it's everything that I prayed and worked hard for it to happen. I didn't know how it was going to turn out but I knew what I wanted and I did the best job I could do for my first album and with the budget I had to deliver.

BK: What about hearing yourself on the radio or seeing yourself on a video channel? What goes through your mind when that happens?

R. KELLY: I'm being born, you know. It's starting to happen, I could feel it. The more I see it, the more people tell me they saw it. The more I get inspired to write another song because I say hey, "I'm gonna be here. I'm doing [it] and it's finally happening."

> Remember, the album is called "Born into the 90's" so he's on point.

BK: Well, what do you think about the fact that maybe, you know, let's say several years ago, people weren't coming up to you, but now they're coming up to you?

R. KELLY: Well, I just think it was my turn, you know, it's my turn. Now several years ago, I was paying my dues, struggling and trying to get here. And now that I've arrived, I plan to stay here for a while because I got music for you know, different artists, not only myself, different styles of music that I do. So I plan to be here for a while, man, you know, I was waiting on my chance to be born into the '90s.

> Back in the day, before cell phones, R. Kelly used to carry a dictaphone so if an idea hit him, he would be able to sing into this pocket-sized recorder, and then run to the studio to record. He actually wrote his first top ten R&B single "She's Got That Vibe" that way. So of course, the young and immature "me" had to talk about his "dick-ta-phone" that he had on the table. I'm not proud of this, but I want to be honest and transparent...let's continue.

BK: Hey, don't bring that dictaphone in front of me. Don't whip out your "dick...ta...phone" with me!

R. KELLY: [laughing] No you won't have to worry about that, your hair not long enough man.

> So I guess I'm happy my hair was short? Or, is he saying I have a chance?!?!? I digress. Please continue "young me" with short hair.

BK: You know another thing you're just sitting here, when you sing in "that vibe," I mean, your voice is pretty pretty stellar. I just don't expect that to come out of you.

R. KELLY: Oh no, man it's me.

BK: Did you always have that voice growing up?

R. KELLY: Yeah, I did. My mother used to have me listening to Marvin Gaye, Stevie Wonder. I met Stevie Wonder the other day [laughs], he was using "the john" man. I couldn't believe, I almost fainted, man. I said, and I don't do this for nobody, I said "Stevie man, I'm R. Kelly. I just got signed with Jive (record label). You my idol man." I said "wait a minute, hold on, I got somethin' I want to show you man, my mother used to make me slow the record up and do this run that you do." And I tried, open my mouth and I laughed at the end of this run but I'm gonna do it. [singing as Stevie Wonder] *Oh, I bet you were someone…put it yesterday to…to let you will be jammin, you will not believe it because you never thought that you will be jammin."*

> His imitation was spot on, he not only sounded like him, he transformed into Stevie Wonder…continue Stevie, I mean Robert.

R. KELLY: So I did this run there, right? And Stevie, you heard him laugh and sniggling a little bit, but I fell into the stall laughing man because I was so frantic. I couldn't even finish the run. But I grew up listening to nothing but Stevie Wonder man. And it was just such an honor to meet him. And I don't care if he was in a john or in a james or whatever. So he said, "aw thanks, thanks man."

BK: That was great Stevie right there, yeah.

R. KELLY: Yeah, I used to imitate Stevie. I was street performing a year and a half ago, two years ago in the subways, up front, on the ground. I had my black glasses and my little keyboard and I be down there doing the Stevie Wonder making a lot of money. You know, singing for people from the nine to fives on Fridays, getting off going to cash that check and bring me a couple of them dollars.

BK: I want to talk about that, you know, there's a very interesting story behind you. You grew up talking about streets, where you know, you're from Chicago. Give me a brief bio of like, where you're from?

R. KELLY: From the Southside of Chicago, I grew up on a little place called 40th Street, where me and my family lived. Like we had the whole house. It was third floor grandmother, second floor sister, first floor me and my mother and brothers and sisters, you know? Yeah. And we knew everybody on the block, that type of thing. Every summer we have barbecue parties and just have fun.

BK: Alright, so we're talking Southside Chicago, rough upbringing in the sense of rough streets, no?

R. KELLY: Yeah. But we got by, you know, me and my family, my mother taught us how to get by. We lived where there was gangs like around the corner. But we knew where to go, where not to go okay? But I was never IN the gangs. I knew gang members and stuff like that, but never into it. One day, I was riding my bike and I got shot. I was 13 and got shot off the bike. Didn't know I was shot, all I was concerned about was the bike my mother spent so much money to buy. I mean, save so much money to buy for me. I look over my shoulder, I'm on the ground, I see three guys rolling off with my bike, you know, that was my main concern at 13, I didn't realize what had happened to me. So my mother and my sister and brother and everybody come rushing over there to me, I mean crying and stuff, you know, telling me what had happened. I've been shot, you know, got me to the hospital and the doctors did not operate because the bullet was too close to a nerve. What they said was, if they operate and it hit the nerve, then it will paralyze my arm. So they just left it alone, because they said tissue at that young age would grow around the bullet and if it ever move, then they would operate. They never operate. So obviously it never moved.

> Despite growing up in a challenging environment, his focus as a child wasn't on the violence but on protecting the simple joys, like his bike—a symbol of his mother's love and sacrifice. And, a great lesson learned.

R. KELLY: It taught me at a young age to first of all, killing and robbing and all that stuff, I don't want to do that. That's not my thing. Also to spread to all the other fellas around me, let's not do that. Let's do something better than that. Let's try to stop that, you know? And it also taught me at a young age to appreciate life you know, and make my decision up and what route I wanted to go at that age.

BK: Talk about a role model, I mean, you're like living proof for a lot of kids out there.

> Okay, remember, this was 1992. There was no crystal ball...No sex tapes...yet. Hindsight is 20-20, and now he's serving 30 in the penitentiary.

R. KELLY: Yeah, I see it's becoming like that which I don't mind man because I'm a good guy you know. *I have nothing to hide. And the things that I want to do is for everybody to love eventually.* This first album is with the kids and with the girls and the guys, it's chilling and everything. And maybe the second album will be similar to that but a little more mature. But you know eventually I want to get into some things that everybody's going to really get into and see R. Kelly and see that his music and him as a friend of everybody's.

BK: I don't mean to go back and back a little bit. But I forgot to ask you a little bit about how you used to be on the street, like you said, Stevie Wonder. Can you talk about that aspect that you used to basically sit out there, a little Casio or whatever it was?

R. KELLY: Yeah well, it started out me and my friends. We went on Rush Street in Chicago. We had nothing to do, just having fun, you know, and I had a little Casio keyboard that I carry around with me. We were hungry. We didn't have any, you know, money on us. Like we have some at home. Who am I kidding? We was broke. We went on Rush Street, a lot of people, exciting, and we'd be like man break out the keyboard man, do something you know. So I had my hat, took the hat off, gave it to Larry. They put it on the sidewalk. I put the glasses on. This is just for fun at this point. I'm playing and singing and stuff. So people started putting money, started off as dimes, nickels, quarters, then people started stopping and really listening to me putting $5 bills, $10 bills, you know? And I said, man, I can't believe this. So I kept singing, kept on singing. Yeahhhhh… and after it was over, we all went and got something to eat man. It was like Robin Hood and his men type of thing, everybody just went and feast, you know? So after that I said man, I think I'm gonna try this. It took me to think about it and get up my nerves and stuff. But hey, I'm a lover of music you know, I love it. It loves me.

BK: You got arrested a couple of times right?

R. KELLY: Yes I did. I was gonna mention that I, you know, I ain't gonna short you. I got arrested three times as a matter of fact. The first time is because I didn't have no license. I didn't know you have to have a license. It was just something I was trying which is understandable you know, uncle Sam got to get his. So I went and got my license. The next two times, don't know what I got arrested for actually, I just got arrested. One cop came up to me and said all right, Stevie, let's go [laughs loud]. Cops get sometimes, they humorous, right? So, I say I got my license Thursday. "That doesn't matter, you're still disturbing the peace." They took me and wrote me a ticket. After they gave me a ticket, they said I don't want to see you anymore. I went right back out there man because they had no reason to stop me. I had my license. I went right back out there, made my money and left. Two weeks later, I went down there and those same cops came and they arrested me again.

BK: Now so basically, you've been arrested, but not for like when people think of people getting arrested, they're thinking for drugs, guns…

R. KELLY: Right?

BK: You got arrested for singing!

R. KELLY: I got arrested for singing with a license, a license to sing. And I really, I really felt discouraged. But see when you discourage me, it's for the better for me, because it only makes me stronger. That's all it does to me.

BK: Must have been some awful singing man. We gotta arrest this guy…

R. KELLY: No, no, no, I was on key and everything. It's echoed down there, it's a good sound, you know, so I was on key. My pitches was straight, but they just arrested me man. To this day, I can't believe and I don't understand why.

BK: You were single-parent raised. How does that affect the way you think to this day, does it affect your music or your view or anything?

R. KELLY: *Nah, you know why man? Cause my mother was everything to me. My mother was father, uncle, brother, sister, friend, everything man. It's almost like it would have been messed up to have a father. So I know one day my father is gonna come and say, "Hey Robert, remember me?" You know, it's coming, maybe after "Honey Love." But uh, my mother was everything to me, man. And I love her. And it didn't affect me at all. I still done all of the things the other kids did, you know?*

BK: What about your family? What do they think of your music? When you said I'm gonna do music, did they say "don't do music, you know, get a real job."

R. KELLY: Well, sometimes some of my family members would say, "well, why don't you just go to school and college and try to get something to fall back on." But I made it up in my mind that I was going to do music. I didn't plan on falling back. So, this is what I knew I wanted, you know, and they still love me even though I made my own decision. You may think at first they may not love you, but once you make your decision, stick to it, they're gonna still love you.

BK: I asked you earlier in the interview, why music and you gave a great answer. Did you know? Like you said, you knew you made a decision, when did you know?

R. KELLY: I actually knew when I went to high school, and I met a lady by the name of Lena McLin. She's the music teacher in school, and it was my first day as a freshman. She inspired me in such a way that I almost thought I was Superman in a humble way, musically. She picked me out of 50 people, the first day of school. We was getting our papers and the notes and she just stopped her class playing the piano. She said that you're going to be the next Stevie Wonder. And I'm looking at her like, "who's this lady talking to me telling me this?"

> Everyone needs a mentor in life. It's better if it's someone outside of the home as a young impressionable teen might not want to take advice from a parent, they usually don't. But Ms. McLin seemed like an angel, the way he speaks about her is truly beautiful. He's not done either.

R. KELLY: So when she told me that, she made me get up in front of the class, put on her glasses, walk around the room. Man, this story is so true and it's coming back to me...walk around the room. It was the most embarrassing point of my whole life, but I thank her for it. I love her for it. Because the key is they laughed, but it was a positive laugh. They was loving what I was singing, which she had me sing, "You Are so Beautiful." Then she gave a talent show at the school, 200 or more kids, and had somebody to get me out there as Stevie Wonder and do "Ribbon in the Sky." Everybody loved it, I won the talent show. I've never in my life looked out into an audience of that many people at the same time seeing them love me. Didn't know me, but they felt me. Because at that time, which I didn't really know, I had something in my voice that could touch people. And it touched them. If it hadn't touched him, they would have just sat there. But they was hooting and hollering, they was loving it.

> Everyone needs a Ms. McLin. I think every record label could use her in their A&R department. He's still not done.

R. KELLY: So from there, she said, you're gonna sing, you're gonna sing for the whole world one day. You're gonna write songs, I want you to start messing with the piano and learning it. I started doing it. And I started learning the piano rapidly, you know, and songs were coming to me from nowhere. I thought I stole a song, you know. I said, "wait a minute, did I write this?" You know, I heard this somewhere before. But then I didn't. It was a song coming to me, which was amazing to sit down to a piano and play it with no lessons, taught myself to play the piano but I was inspired by her. I was so inspired by her, she started taking me to operas and malls. I'd clean up her house while she played the piano and I just started getting the spirit about me from her. She would sit in front of my face and write a whole song, and tell me that I'm gonna do the same thing one day for the world.

BK: And you're doing it.

R. KELLY: And I'm doing it. And she was so inspiring that if she told me to go pick up a building, I feel like at least I'd go budge it. That's how inspired I was by this lady. She told me I will go through a whole lot of trials and tribulations before I would make it, and I have been through 'em.

> Okay, see what I mean?!?! He was fantastic, and the only thing he got arrested for was singing...at that time. I know I know...he's been arrested since, and it wasn't for singing which brings me to this next little item. I had been sitting on an interview I did with Aaliyah from May of 1994 for her debut album in which R. Kelly wrote and produced all the songs. You can check out my conversation with Aaliyah a little later in this book, as she was definitely one of my favorites and one of my classics. She is no longer with us, as she was tragically killed in an airplane accident in the Bahamas in 2001, at the age of 22. Too young...which is a theme in R. Kelly's troubles. But keep in mind, Aaliyah's debut album was titled "Age Ain't Nothing But A Number." Still, when I interviewed her, she alluded to the fact that she was young when she met Robert, but credits him for her initial success. Here's the quote:

BK: So let me ask you how you actually hooked up with R. Kelly in the first place. I mean, everyone would love to meet a guy like him right, have him take them under the wing. Was that your big break?

AALIYAH: That was because that's when everything came together. And that's when it really started for this album...I met him three years ago. I'm not gonna tell you how old [coughs and laughs].

> Okay, when you hear the tape it's clear she was joking about how young she was. Continue please.

AALIYAH: But I met him when he was just completing *Born into the 90's* through our manager, because we had the same manager. And I auditioned for him. I sang "Get Here" by Oleta Adams and he liked it. And then we started working on a couple of songs, and we got close over the years. And we did this album this past year, in '93 that was it.

So I get why this may be sort of controversial, with R. Kelly in prison for doing bad things. But musically, there are many examples of courting "young love" that by today's standards are beyond creepy. I will give you two from artists who I have met and interviewed.

Keith Sweat

His song "Right And Wrong Way" is an ode to young, inappropriate love. I won't include ALL of the lyrics, but he gets right to the point in the first verse:

My, my, my, my, my, my baby
You're mine, mine, mine, mine
I'm gonna love you right, girl
You may be young but you're ready
(Ready to learn)
You're not a little girl, you're a woman

Wow, but that's not all. He ends the song with a sentiment that confirms my theory:

We'll love each other eternally, just you and me, baby
Oh, oh, oh
You're a big girl now (there's a good and a bad way to love somebody)
No more daddy's little girl.

Okay, not calling Keith out as I am a fan, but just giving you a historical perspective of R&B at the time.

Benny Mardones

My second example is even more overt in its creepy sentiment, but at the time no one complained. It was 1980 and Benny Mardones released "Into The Night" which was a love song to a 16-year-old when he was 34 years old. Here's a sample of the opening lyrics:

She's just 16 years old
Leave her alone, they said
Separated by fools
Who don't know what love is yet
But I want you to know
If I could fly
I'd pick you up
I'd take you into the night
And show you a love
Like you've never seen, ever seen

Okay, not okay, but if you really want to creep out then watch the original video as it's literally acted out in real time. I can't make this up, just giving you a perspective of the arc of inappropriateness.

I don't excuse what R. Kelly is behind bars for—of course not. But when I met him in the prime of his career, he had the right mix of charm and immense talent. The entertainment industry and the public recognized it, though both can be brutal on a pop star. I witnessed that firsthand at one of my "radio rows" for the Billboard Awards.

I was beyond thrilled when R. Kelly agreed to talk to a group of my invited radio stations while promoting his latest project. The record label asked if interviewers could stick to music and avoid any of the allegations circulating at the time. He was HUGE, and I promised to make that happen—everyone wanted to talk to him because he rarely did press. But when I greeted him, he wasn't the same bubbly, excited artist I had met just a few years earlier.

Radio was eager to interview the elusive star, but some on-air personalities just can't help themselves. One station ignored the agreement and repeatedly pressed him about Aaliyah and other accusations. I was told that Robert politely declined to answer—three times. Then, when they pushed him again, he flipped. And I mean, flipped—the table.

I was across the room and ran over when I heard what happened. And I was pissed—not at Robert, but at the DJs. The record label wasn't happy either. They grabbed Robert and left. Meanwhile, the DJ thought it was funny. It wasn't.

I equate it to today's social media culture—people being provocative just for clicks. Sensationalism drives engagement, but at what cost? If those DJs really wanted more listeners, they could have asked the right questions—about his music, his inspirations (Stevie Wonder, Ms. McLin, his mother). Those were the things that made R. Kelly light up. And just maybe—just maybe—they might have gotten him to sing, like he did for me. That would have been a classic interview. A classic conversation.

ANITA BAKER

WHEN YOU CAN'T FIND YOUR PICTURE WITH TONI, YOU INCLUDE A SIGNED AUTOGRAPH WITH ONE OF HER BIGGEST INFLUENCES, ANITA BAKER. "NO WORRIES."

MEETING TONI BRAXTON IS A MEMORABLE EXPERIENCE THAT STANDS OUT IN MY CAREER.
It's interesting how certain moments leave a lasting impression, while others fade away over time. It was at the Le Montrose hotel in West Hollywood in a conference room on the ground floor. I remember because it took a minute to find her as her label representative wasn't there and I didn't know what she looked like. And when I did meet her, she wasn't wearing makeup or stylish clothes, I wasn't either.

I didn't have a full-fledged bio or much information on Toni as LaFace was a relatively new record label, and I was interviewing her for the soundtrack singles for the Eddie Murphy movie *Boomerang*. Her songs were on the radio, so I needed to get the stories. I recall listening to the music and thinking "this is pretty pretty good," what a unique voice. It was earthy, sultry, low, definitely different from what pop and R&B radio were playing at the time. It's almost as if Toni took voice lessons from Anita Baker, another distinctive soulful singer. That voice—I needed to meet this woman!

Leave it to L.A. Reid & Babyface to tap her to sing the demos for the singles on the soundtrack, and for the film's director Reginald Hudlin's choice to approve her. What a soundtrack, the music was not only integral to the film, but it was also a moneymaker for the label selling over three million copies. Huge for a soundtrack that also had Boyz II Men's "End of The Road" which was at the top of the charts that day.

There's a lot of chats I don't recall, but as I stated in the beginning, I definitely remember having a classic conversation with Toni.

BK: Test 1-2-3. So I want you to feel free to open up to me, come on Toni. Open up to us. Say hello.

TONI: Hello. No, Hi. How are you?

BK: I'm doing well. And you? A big year for you, right? Kinda..

TONI: Kind of, maybe on its way, I hope.

BK: What I meant by what a year, well, first of all, you know I write one of these pop shows. Been writing about you, like for days, like months.

TONI: Really?

BK: Yeah.

TONI: That's good to hear.

BK: Isn't that nice? Yeah, got that song on the radio!

TONI: "Love Shoulda" or Babyface's. Yeah, it's on the radio.

> "Give U My Heart" was the first single, "Love Shoulda Brought You Home" the second.

BK: Yeah, let's start talking about that. It's still on the radio all the time.

TONI: Yeah, that's good for me and Face.

BK: I'm with you, let's say you hear it today. I mean, in fact, I think I've heard it this morning. What goes through your mind when you hear it right now?

TONI: First of all, when I hear it I'm like, okay, maybe just something different this time so I listen to hear a different way. It never sounds different. And it's personal for me because this is my first opportunity working with L.A. and Face. So we kind of you know, it hits me. Oh, God this is the song that made it happen.

BK: What is it about the song that actually you think people just really got into?

TONI: Um, I guess just Face, I think whenever Face sings a duet with the person, it gets the attention automatically right away. And it wasn't a slow song, it was a fast song so I mean, the dance beat, we got to dance a little bit too you know, "gave me my heart."

> Toni sings it sort of, but not in key and I couldn't let it go.

BK: So how's it go again?

TONI: Not the way I was just singing it. [laughs]

BK: I remember the song.

TONI: It goes [singing it beautifully] "I will gave you my heart, and I will always be true to you."

> Toni's snapping along. I'm grooving, and Toni notices.

TONI: See, you got the beat. You wanna do Face's part?

[Toni laughs]

BK: I think your part's harder right?

TONI: I don't know. Nah, not really.

BK: Alright, when you and Face started singing, when he brought the song, did you have any clue what was going to happen?

TONI: Well they had to submit the songs to Paramount for *Boomerang* and I did the demo for it.

BK: Did you know you nailed it? Like did you feel it?

TONI: I felt it when I sung it. It was like, this is for me. But it may not be so don't get your hopes up, but it happened.

> That is the truth, there are countless horror stories in the entertainment industry of getting the part, not getting the part. Getting the single, not releasing the single. What I didn't know at the time was that she had already been signed to Arista Records with her sisters (before any Braxton fame), they did release music and it didn't go anywhere and they were dropped. So looking back, she had to protect herself and not get her hopes too high.

BK: Beautiful. All right, last thing about the song, just in general, what do you think the song is saying? Kind of says it in the title.

TONI: It says it. I will give you my heart. It says what

it means. I mean, we're pronouncing that part, right? You can hear us on that part, right?

> She's funny.

BK: Oh, yeah..

TONI: Okay, I'll give you my heart. I'll be true to you, you know. I'm a good lady and you're a good guy.

BK: Yeah thanks, Toni.

TONI: Make it happen. [Toni laughs loud, getting BK humor]

BK: I'm a nice guy.

TONI: Yeah, I think you are, you seem like it.

BK: Sure I am *(just ask me)*.

TONI: Oh, sure. Okay,

> In reading the transcript in this exchange, it seems like I was flirting with her. But when listening to the audio, I was trying to make Friday fun for the both of us. And, fun usually translates into better interview, better conversation.

BK: I know you also, as we speak here, you're releasing another record. Can we talk about *"Love Should Have Brought You Home?"* Tell me about that song. What's the story behind that song?

TONI: L.A. and Face wrote it, did a demo. I submitted it. But while doing the demo, I was like, I like the song… so true. I mean, I've never lived with a man so I can't say that, you know, but there were times like people I dated should have been home that night to call me and they were out. You know, where they should have been there at 8:30 to pick me up and not 10 o'clock or two o'clock... So I felt that song I sang, I was like "this is so true." Geez, not just for women, though you know? It's for men. Everybody's experienced it sometime in their life.

BK: Toni, you let me know who did it. I'll come...

TONI: Yeah, I'm gonna write his name down. Take care of it for me.

BK: I'll start smacking him. TONI: Right.

BK: Alright actually as we speak, we get a good song out of it.

TONI: Yeah, a good song came out of it.

> A hit song. What I didn't know at the time was that Babyface and crew wrote the song for Anita Baker who passed on the opportunity as she was pregnant at the time. So when I said her voice sounded like Anita Baker gave her lessons, L.A. Reid and Face felt the same—great ears think alike.

BK: All right, we'll talk about the video, I know you did a video yesterday. What was it like?

TONI: I feel really good about this video. Singing, you know, why didn't you come home last night? I don't want to hear anything else you have to say, that's it you know? It was definitely emotional. You'll see it, trust me. And I hope you enjoy it.

BK: It's got that *Boomerang* vibe.

TONI: Yeah, it's that big scene where Halle [Berry] says to Eddie [Murphy], "love should have brought you, what you [slap bap bap bap] home last night." So the big slap comes about there.

BK: Did you like the movie?

TONI: Loved the movie. I love the movie. Not because [laughs] LaFace has the soundtrack, but I thought it was a very entertaining movie.

BK: I know because I've read, but how did you hook up with these guys, L.A. Reid and Babyface?

TONI: Well, it's kind of like a long story but I'm gonna summarize it. So when I was younger, my background was very strict. So I wasn't allowed to listen to secular music like the radio, you know things and such. So my parents would leave, I turn, you know listen to the radio. I'd listen to Quincy Jones, Chaka Khan, the remake of Michael Jackson "Gotta Be There," Stevie Wonder's "Someone you Love," the *Songs* project I never knew. So I sneaked, listened to 'em more. I'd sneak in my Soul Train, my parents weren't up on a Saturday. I got caught once but I listened to it, you know. Slowly but surely my parents started changing gradually. And by the time I got to high school, you know, it started becoming okay to listen to music. You could turn it up a little more. I have younger sisters and they're like you couldn't listen to music? What, why? They can't understand it.

> How funny is that? Toni's parents were so strict about secular music that, under their rules, she wouldn't have been allowed to listen to her own songs. Shout out to her talented sisters, though, who didn't have to sneak around to enjoy or perform the music they loved! So Toni started performing—wait, I will let her sum up.

TONI: I used to sing locally…and I met some local producers and through local producers I met Bill Pettaway. I don't know if you know Bill Pettaway, but I will refresh you. He wrote "Girl You Know It's True" by Milli Vanilli. And through him I met Ernesto Phillips from Starpoint and through Ernesto Phillips from Starpoint, I went to Arista and through Arista, that's how L.A. and Face became aware of me.

> Toni's journey to becoming the icon we know today is a testament to how music can ignite passion and defy expectations. She didn't let her parents' doubts about what she should enjoy hold her back. Instead, she embraced her creative spirit, proving that once passion takes hold, it's impossible to ignore. Even an unexpected break with the creative team behind Milli Vanilli shows that success often blends hard work, talent, and a little bit of luck. Her story reminds us that following what moves you can open doors you never imagined.
>
> Funny '90s hip hop side note–when I was interviewing the Beastie Boys for their *Paul's Boutique* record, I gave them the opportunity to be guest DJs for a syndicated radio show. And who did they choose to spin? Yes, Milli Vanilli.

BK: A lot of people want to meet these guys because they're hot hip happening producers. But what did they see in you?

TONI: I had to do a showcase for them. And I played some songs I'd written and sung and danced a little bit. And it's just like a hit, the chemistry was there. So, it was like one of those thangs.

BK: One of those thangs. I've interviewed a lot of

people who work with LaFace. So tell me what are these guys like? Let's start with Babyface.

TONI: He is great. He's a bit reserved until you know, he warms up to you. And then he's very witty, charming, of course, you know. Our favorite pastime with him is getting five dollars worth of quarters and playing Ms. Pac-Man, which he always wins. I haven't beat him yet. But he's very serious when it comes to his music and he's this nice, very nice guy.

BK: One of the best things that he said, I remember I asked a question about his writing, I said, "What do you write?" He said "I write from the heart."

TONI: Definitely. Definitely all day long, he writes from the heart. Which is good. I mean, it works obviously.

BK: What did you learn? Well, let's talk about L.A.

TONI: L.A. is great. He has his way, both of them. But L.A. was bringing your music out on the tape. He was narrating the story through your voice, you know, because some songs like "Love Should Have Brought You Home," do you sing it soft? Or do you sing like, legitimate you're angry? So they're both great with that but they're just great guys and very warm. And, they take care of me, meaning they make sure everything's okay. "Toni, what do you need?" You know? "How is your music coming along?" Like father figures. Definitely father figures.

BK: What did you get from working with them? From their style, you know the things that you still think about just from watching them or dealing with them?

TONI: That it's important, I mean Face is the singer of the group. So sometimes it was one of the demos, Face singing. And they're like Face is singing this, but sing it your way. So that's important. Oh my God, it's Babyface and you become intimidated. But like sing it your way, sing it the way you want to sing it, ignore Babyface. Don't try to sing it like him. He just said to demo, do your stuff. And you learn.

BK: Which brings me to another question Toni Braxton. When you get a song from these guys, how do you put what makes it a Toni Braxton song besides the obvious putting your voice on it?

TONI: I think that when I sing, I'm an aggressive singer…I mean, certain parts of the song I'll be a little timid, soft, but I'm an aggressive singer. And that's what makes it Toni Braxton. I mean, every song you can't be aggressive on. But I think my voice stands out a little more. A little more powerful.

BK: What are you like in the studio with these guys? You know, describe yourself in the studio.

TONI: Their patience, that's what I love. They're patient because I'm a new artist, and a lot of things are new to me, developing my skills. I belong, and they've been very patient with me.

BK: Do you ever feel like oh my god, I can't believe I'm doing this?

TONI: Oh, all the time. Like I am standing next to L.A. Reid and Babyface. Oh my god, they're talking to me you know…sometimes it's hard to believe it.

BK: You're like "Hey, this isn't that bad." Do you feel the pressure?

TONI: Um, originally I did. It's like okay, this is L.A. and Face. They worked with, first of all, they're the greatest producers, two of the greatest producers. And they work with Whitney Houston, who's my favorite singer, Bobby Brown. You know, all these great people. They've worked with Johnny Gill, I'm like, you know, why me? You know, it's hard to believe that but it's flattering, but it's like, I hope I'm as good as they are.

BK: Tell me something, are they producing your debut record?

TONI: We just started on the album. So we haven't picked all the songs yet. But I just did a song last week, they produced the mix last night, which is a great song. So maybe that's gonna be it.

BK: What's it called?

TONI: It's called "Another Sad Love Song." And it's about when you break up with the person and you're in your car, what do you hear? A sad love song all the time. So it's about that.

BK: I hate that.

TONI: Don't you hate that? All the time.

> So here's the deal on what I used to do for a living—I loved conversating which is a word, I didn't think so but Warren G (name drop) said it in my interview and I was laughing inside thinking it wasn't a word, but it is! But I digress.
>
> I loved talking to creatives about a project, a movie, TV show, or upcoming song and then BOOM, it's out and becomes a huge hit with critics and the public. That's what happened with Toni's debut single from her debut album. It's one of my favorites.

> "Another Sad Love Song" earned Braxton her first-ever Grammy Award for Best Female R&B Vocal Performance at the 36th Annual Grammy Awards and I was there backstage to congratulate her and give her a big fat hug! Back to the conversation.

BK: Alright well, a lot of people might not know who Toni Braxton is. We're gonna tell them right now. So Toni, do me a favor. Give me like a little brief bio. I know you're from DC, but you know, can you tell us like, you know, where are you from? And...

TONI: I'm actually, I'm from Maryland. I grew up in Southern Maryland. And I graduated from high school, went to college, and I went to Bowie State University. I lived in Greenbelt, Maryland...and I've been living there until I just moved down to Atlanta, three months ago. What a wonderful, wonderful world of music.

BK: Growing up in Maryland, did you have any clue that you'd be singing? Obviously, you probably sang in the church...

TONI: Of course.

BK: It's a given.

TONI: Yeah.

BK: How were you back then?

TONI: How was I?

BK: Yeah. Were you shining above everybody else?

TONI: No, no, not at all. Not at all. I mean, yeah, I would sing. But I was kind of shy...I was always different. So people didn't like me.

BK: Why are you different?

TONI: Because of my background. I was always different. And I always wanted to be a part of the peers and on occasions when they were in good moods, they let me be a part. But I was always different…I'm a big girl now I can handle it.

BK: You tell them, "how do you like me now?"

TONI: [Chuckles] Really.

> The next question is part of a series when I used to ask artists to reflect on the music of the '60s, and if there was a song from that era that brought them back to a moment, a memory. It usually elicits a cool response, and Toni didn't disappoint.

BK: So when you hear a song like "The Way to San Jose," what goes through your mind?

TONI: I was thinking my childhood memories. I used to sing it because I heard it on a commercial. You know, greatest hits by Dionne Warwick and that one stood outside [singing] "do you know the way to San Jose," and I sing it, with a ketchup bottle in the bathroom, it was my microphone. And my toiletries were my audience, you know? [laughs]

BK: Like a hair brush?

TONI: But they just, they listen to me, always listen. I didn't have a dog. So my toiletries did it for me. [laughs]

> Now, she's hilarious—talk about painting a picture. I'm thinking toothbrush, toothpaste, some soap, lotion, Q-tips—she had a packed house. Ketchup bottle? The normal "go-to" fake microphone is a hairbrush, but Toni was an original.

BK: When did you actually know that you can do it? Like really, like do it, do what you're doing, singing.

TONI:

Well, you'll laugh at this...when I was younger, I had a crush on JJ from Good Times. I love myself some JJ. I'm really—this is the true story. But I liked him when Janet Jackson, Penny on the show, when she was on the show. She was a little older, so she likes JJ, I like JJ. So she sung the song on one particular episode, she and Michael Evans sung "You Don't Have To Be A Star Baby, To Be On My Show." So I say, I'm gonna memorize that song so I can sing it to JJ. So I didn't go out, I just listened to it—and I still don't know the words to it. I just know the hook.

BK: [singing, albeit poorly] You don't have to be a star baby.

TONI: [laughs] I wanted to be with JJ.

> This is no longer an interview, it's a conversation and a fun one at that. What a story, JJ was a character, his catchphrase was "Dyn-O-Mite," said with some original swagger from a 6'1" beanpole. Go Toni...

BK: Who knew *Good Times* would have that effect?

TONI: It did. It really did. I thought JJ was so cool when he said "chello." I just thought he was the guy.

> Oh yeah, JJ said "chello" too. I have to hand it to Toni, she was more into personality than looks which gives guys like me a chance.

BK: Music of today, who's out there that's doing it? You just let me know what you like.

TONI: I like everybody; Whitney Houston, my favorite singer in the whole wide world, Anita Baker I love. Babyface of course. Kenny Loggins, I love his voice. George Michael, there's so many guys, so many great great people out there. I love TLC….I love Janet Jackson, Eddie Murphy. I do like Eddie Murphy's voice. I think he's underrated as a singer. I think he's a very good singer.

BK: Have you ever heard me sing?

TONI: Oh, no. You're gonna…go ahead and sing for me.

BK: [singing] Do you know the way to San…

TONI: [laughing]

> This is where I should have said Dyn-O-Mite!

BK: You know I'm a songwriter?

TONI: Oh, really? You have a song for me?

BK: Yeah, it's called Happy Birthday. You know how it goes?

TONI: No, let me hear it.

BK: [singing and snapping to the classic childhood ditty] Happy birthday to you.

TONI: Oh, okay. Got it.

BK: Alright, fine. You don't like my humor.

TONI: It's okay. You know, I understand… you can't be funny all the time.

> Chello?

BK: Are you gonna be touring? Are you going to want to get out there?

TONI: That's my favorite part. I hate studio. Oh, God, I hate studio. I hate that part. I love singing live, it's a great feeling, great feeling.

BK: Last question is the future for Toni Braxton. What's going to happen? What would you like to see happen?

TONI: Gosh, just have a great album. platinum album. Maybe some Grammys in the future? I don't know, it's hard to say…Just having great music and making everyone happy and enjoying it.

And there you have it. Talk about predicting the future, she could be like Dionne Warwick and have the new Psychic Friends Network (I crack myself up).

Let's recap. She said:

"Great Album, Platinum Album." Check and check! Most critics had a positive take on her debut, and the fans rewarded her with a number one album and worldwide sales of over 10 million copies. That's enough platinum to fill up Lil Wayne's entire mouth.

"Maybe some Grammys in the future?" Check, check and check. Her debut album earned Braxton three Grammy Awards including the highly coveted Best New Artist.

"Just having great music and making everyone happy and enjoying it."

Checkmate!

Toni Braxton has earned her place among the greats— Whitney, Janet, and yes, Anita. Looking back at our 1992 conversation, I was reminded of her charm, talent, and the "good times" she brought to R&B. I hope you had as much fun reading it as I did reliving it.

A DJ, A FRESH PRINCE, AND A LEGEND WALK INTO THE '90S

MY RELATIONSHIP WITH WILL SMITH GOES BACK TO 1989—let me rephrase, my "professional" relationship. We weren't dating. We weren't friends. He was an up-and-coming multi-threat artist, and I was just a member of the entertainment press, covering his rise.

I interviewed him one-on-one in 1989, 1991, and 1993—first for his music and television show, then as he skyrocketed into movies. I was there for his box-office takeover, interviewing him at press junkets for *Six Degrees of Separation*, *Bad Boys*, *Independence Day*, *Men in Black*, and more. Will was beyond likable, effortlessly funny, and—just as he appeared to the public—completely at ease in his own skin. Watching him transform from rapper to Fresh Prince to global movie star, I couldn't have been happier for him.

So why is Will Smith a classic conversation? Simple. He was a great performer in interviews. And by that, I mean he made my job easy. Will didn't just answer questions—he delivered soundbites before I even finished asking. His energy was infectious, his timing impeccable. And when he was paired with DJ Jazzy Jeff, it was even better. Those two reminded me of the Bee Gees—not musically, but in the way they cracked each other up in interviews. They had a rhythm, a chemistry. The kind that makes any conversation fun.

There's a reason Will made it to the top of the fame mountain. And I was lucky to witness the early days of his climb.

For this particular interview, the focus was on the new album, *Code Red*. I met him at the Beverly Hilton, at the corner of Wilshire and Santa Monica boulevards. No assistant. No manager. No "team" of publicists. Just Will, in his hotel room.

He's a classic—and here's some of our conversation.

BK: I'm sure you're talking about everything. Will, I want to talk about *Code Red*.

WILL: *Code Red*.

BK: Do you remember what that is?

WILL: *Code Red*, that's the brand new album by Jazzy Jeff and the Fresh Prince for 1993, spanking new.

BK: Unbelievable. I hear you. It's the fifth album for you.

WILL: Right, the fifth album. That's kind of a good point for us. Because the fifth album is pretty much uncharted territory for rap music. If you can make it to five albums, that means you're definitely doing something right. So you know, we're a little nervous about this and we want this to be successful. This is an extremely important album for us. And it's an album to watch in the scope of rap music in general.

> It's funny, *Code Red* ended up being their final album as a duo.

BK: It's your new baby. Outside of the movies and your TV, what's your feelings on the album as a whole?

WILL: I think *Code Red*, track for track, is the best album that we've ever done. This album has the most eclectic taste that a couple of brothers could put together. This album is different from anything that we've done. It's more dance oriented. It's more up-tempo. Poetically, I stepped up a couple notches on this album, I think more like seasoned veterans of the genre.

BK: Now there's definitely an obvious growth there and you talk about the wide mix. What was going on?

WILL: Well, what happened? I think the way that we got so many different style tracks on the album is because it took us two years to do it. And in the course of two years, you run through a whole different style of emotions and a whole different feeling, a whole different attitude. So just everything in your life changes. So while you're writing songs, you're writing about totally different things. And I was a totally different person from the time I wrote the first track to the time I wrote the last. So all of these different things went into play. But the album came out real good. I'm happy with it.

BK: What about as far as you even alluded to the fact that you're out, like, on the weekends, promoting it and trying. I mean, an album can suffer because you have so much on your plate.

WILL: Oh, I know yeah.

BK: I mean this in the nicest way...

WILL: Yeah I think that in the minds of the fans in America, they like the separation between the artists. They like the separation of an actor from a musician and the separation from a movie personality to a television personality. So overseas, they don't mind if things are crossed a little bit. If people do all the other different things, there's not really a backlash to that.

BK: What about as far as the creative process on this record? In fact, I talked to you and Jazzy a couple times, you know, for the last album and before that. You talked about when you were doing your shows, it was a different creative process, coast to coast. How did it work on this record?

WILL: Well, Jeff is working on a TV show. So he's out in LA with me a lot and we have a chance to work on different stuff. I had a studio in my house, and we knocked tracks out. So it was a little easier working on this album than the last one.

BK: Was there anything specific, though? Like, because when you guys start putting songs together, and start doing it, is there anything specific that you want *Code Red* to be, any direction you were going?

WILL: No, we never plan. We never plan a direction. Before we work on an album, we just make songs and see what happens. And then after you get seven or eight songs, you'll feel a void. And once you feel a void, then you fill it, you know, you might make 10 songs and you say, "You know what, all of these songs are slow. We need some up tempo tracks." And then that's when you start to make it a point.

BK: What about your rapping skills? Do you keep it, do you have to practice? What do you do?

WILL: I don't think that you ever really need to practice because it's something that you've done for so long. The practice comes in the performance, and you just kind of need to get back up to speed. What we'd like to do, like before our last album, we just went and did 10 shows in Japan to prepare to do shows in the states and that's kind of how you just get your skill level back up.

> Will Smith is BIG in Japan. So am I, kind of...you have to love that they go to Japan to get back into the groove, get jiggy if you will. It's like they can fail, and no one would know. I equate this to comedians doing small clubs testing out material before they do their Netflix special.

BK: Well, staying on the music because I'm strictly on music here. I know about...you know, you're a daddy and all that stuff. (And all that stuff?) I don't think I talked to you since you become a daddy. How does that, or does it affect the music? I'm sure it affects your life.

WILL: Yeah, it doesn't really affect the music, having a son, because I've always made music that people's kids can listen to anyway. It doesn't change anything that I think or I feel in the studio. The only barometer

I've ever used is my parents. I want my parents to be proud of the stuff that I make. You know, if they're sitting at work, and my stuff comes on the radio, I want them to be proud that that's their son.

BK: Now, that's very nice to say. However, in this day and age, that doesn't necessarily happen all the time. Maybe with your music, yes, but what are your feelings on the hardcore? I mean, you've been asked this question, I even asked you before.

WILL: As far as the hardcore rap, that's just, that's not what I do. I like listening to it. I see the beauty of Ice Cube, I see the beauty of Ice-T, NWA, Dr. Dre., Snoop Dogg. It's not every single lyric that they say, I mean every once in a while everybody's gonna say something that you disagree with. But for the most part, I respect other artists to do what they want to do. The only time that I feel any negative vibes about it is when I think it's somebody that's not saying something that they truly mean, you know? I don't think I've ever heard Ice Cube say something that I didn't feel that he meant.

BK: After meeting Ice Cube I agree…What about as far as you know, in fact, I've done a little bit more preparation than usual, I read a couple of the articles written about you after this role. Any worry about perception in the rap community?

WILL: The Six Degrees role?

> I was alluding to Will's big-screen breakthrough role in *Six Degrees of Separation*, where he plays a smooth-talking con artist who tricks his way into the world of Manhattan's elite by posing as Sidney Poitier's son. His character—a gay man—invites a hustler to a swanky Fifth Avenue apartment, the façade crumbles, and all hell breaks loose.
>
> Back in the early '90s, the rap community wasn't as open to LGBQT issues or movies for that matter.

WILL: Early before I took the role I was worrying about how would it affect the music, how would it affect the television show and my career in general.

And the bottom line is just to do good work. That's my bottom line. I do good work. Anytime you do good work, it's beyond any racial bounds or any other boundaries that someone will try to put around artists. If it's good, everybody can accept it.

> I love this message, the simple wisdom, the masterclass of a work ethic. I also felt (and feel) it's important to highlight how people and critics were concerned about being "gay" or even portraying a "gay character" in certain communities, not just ones of color. I think it's amazing how far we've come as a society where the majority of folks don't care what you are, who you love, or how you live.

BK: Let's talk about Code Red for a second, the significance, I mean, it's a great title of an album when I saw it. Oh, there's a song there too. Yeah. Can you just talk about your feelings on that whole aspect?

WILL: Well, in the record what a "code red" is, is a warning. Basically the way we use that, you know, we're hanging out, if you're talking to some girl or something like that, and your girlfriend walks in, that's a "code red," you know, "Yo, man code red." You know, and so that was something that we were using just acting stupid. So we did the record about it. But I think that that is the closest to the old Jazzy Jeff and Fresh Prince flavor that we have on the album that's, you know, close to the "I Think I Can Beat Mike Tyson" and "Parents Just Don't Understand," "Girls Ain't Nothing But Trouble" all those kinds of records.

> Again, no one worried about hardcore lyrics or sentiments here.

BK: Looking back you know…

WILL: I just can't believe how high my voice was when I

listened to those old records. You know, I was 16 and 17 years old making those records. And I'm 25 now and my voice has changed and all of that. And it just cracks me up to hear the old stuff.

BK: Well, it sounds like you're moving in the right direction. In other words, there's a great quote from you, in one of these articles I read about the sight of an aging rapper. It's just not a pretty sight. [Will laughs]

> Cue the irony. In March of 2025, 56-year-old Will Smith released his first full-length album in over 20 years, called *Based on a True Story*. 56 is the new 26. I am not judging, just relaying what he said about aging rappers.
>
> Back to the interview.

BK: Yet you're still in production, you still on TV and you're doing, you know, a movie role. Can you talk, it seems like you have some type of plan here. Maybe?

WILL: Yeah, I don't know if I really have an overall career plan. I just have the philosophy to do good work, just consistently do good work. This is a difficult period because now that I've done a couple of films, people want to throw a lot of money at you. And it gets exciting. And you don't want to do subpar work because the amount of money, you know. And it's going to be difficult to find the level of role in movies that I want to do, you know? It's like after Six Degrees, that was the pinnacle experience, that was the epitome of every aspect of filmmaking. It was a great script with a great writer with a brilliant director and Stockard Channing and Donald Sutherland, it's like everything lined up perfectly on that one. So I was kind of concerned with the next role, I want to make sure the next role is definitely up to the challenge.

> Safe to opine here that with multiple nominations and wins in acting, and many memorable performances (*Ali* my fav), his overall career plan seemed to work.

BK: Last question…a fluff question, it's the typical like, is life good? You know from the outside everyone imagines you have a charm about your life, seems to be. Can you talk about life for Will Smith?

WILL: Yeah, life…life is definitely good. Life is difficult. Now there's not enough hours in the day to do all the things that I want to do. Trying to hold down three careers that are all happening at once. To have the television show out, a new movie coming out and an album out at the same time is…[pauses, thinking] you know, rough. It's kind of rough on the body and then trying to do things around the world and flying and all of that. So life is definitely good. I wouldn't trade it for anything.

BK: Done.

WILL: All right. Oh, thank you, sir. Thank you.

He was—and still is—a true superstar. Affable, lovable, and all that… until the slap heard around the world in 2022.

What's funny to me about that Oscars night is that I was rooting for him to win. I had even voted for him a few months earlier in my own awards show, the *Critics Choice Awards*, where he took home Best Actor and delivered an amazing acceptance speech. In a rare move for me, I even posted a video on social media the morning of the Academy Awards, wishing him luck. Well… that post didn't age well.

Will won the battle (the trophy) but lost the war. His actions in defending his wife didn't land nearly as well as the shot to comedian Chris Rock's face.

Still, my conversations with him were classic—long before Jada, Jaden, Willow, or any Red Table Talk. Like I said at the beginning, my "relationship" with Will Smith goes back to 1989. And at his core, I know he's a good person. A talented creative.

America, and the world, love a redemption story. And I think there's still a chance for this one to have a happy ending.

Because really—who doesn't love a happy ending?

Sheldon Reynolds Andrew Woolfolk Sonny Emory Verdine White
Ralph Johnson Philip Bailey Maurice White

EARTH, WIND & FIRE

I NEVER NEED AN EXCUSE TO INCLUDE A PICTURE OF MAURICE WHITE IN A BOOK ABOUT HIP HOP AND R&B, BUT HAMMER MAN GAVE ME THE OPPORTUNITY TO DO SO COURTESY OF HIS COLLABORATION WITH EWF.

I KNOW I HAVE CHOSEN SOME OF THE BIGGER NAMES IN MUSIC AS "CLASSIC CONVERSATIONS,"

and I had to check myself before I wrecked myself to make sure I wasn't doing this consciously or subconsciously. But with MC Hammer, I think it's beyond worthy because at the time I was interviewing him in early '94, he wasn't at the top of the music food chain where he had been residing just a few years earlier.

I remember seeing him perform at his peak—a sold out show at The Great Western Forum in Los Angeles, where Hammer was literally "Too Legit To Quit." It was the summer of '92, and I had just interviewed all of his opening acts (Boyz II Men, TLC, Jodeci) so going to the concert was "work" for me. MC Hammer was the ultimate showman, and with a dozen backup dancers, a dozen backup singers, and a 12-piece band, they were the dirty dozens of performances. I honestly don't remember exact head counts but let's just say he brought new meaning to the term entourage.

By then, his relationship with Capitol Records seemed to be souring, along with his taste for the industry grind. The entertainment world can be brutal: first building an artist up to the top, then reveling in their fall.

But that wasn't me, I wasn't critiquing him or his music, I was just an ally in publicity and promotion and excited to be on the team. This was my first time interviewing the rap star, as all I had done up to this point was talk to him backstage at multiple awards shows where he was celebrating wins and answering questions like "How does it feel to win a Grammy?" Yuck, I might have asked him that several times but I digress...as usual.

We met to talk about his album, *The Funky Headhunter*, a new release on a new label. I was a little too focused on his return to the spotlight as he "was" MC Hammer and now he dropped the MC to become Hammer, or Hammer Man. Honestly, call him whatever you want but his music was fun and delivered a massive dose of positivity. As I listened back to the audio, I felt like I was listening to the ultimate life coach. So, without further ado, let's "Turn This Mutha Out." Sorry about that, but I felt that the lyric has more gravitas than "Let's Get It Started."

BK: A new single, a new Hammer, is it a new Hammer?

HAMMER: It's a new Hammer from the standpoint of a more aggressive Hammer, you know, a funkier sound from that aspect.

BK: What brought about the more aggressive Hammer?

HAMMER: The times...this is '94. You know, you have to be more aggressive in life in general. This is not laid back '90s...'90s you have to go out and get it man. So this is like the Hammer from a different aspect.

BK: Well, tell us about "It's All Good." I mean, when I first heard it, it's heavy funk, it just comes right at you. It's pounding. And it's all good, you know? Head bobbing. Can you talk about that aspect?

HAMMER: Well yeah. The energy and aggressiveness that you

feel and that you hear "It's All Good" is a reflection of, you know, my character. *And what the record is really talking about is that no matter what comes in your way, or what somebody might have to say, remember, no matter what, they can't stop you. It's all good.*

> Life Coach Lesson #1

BK: I can tell you can relate to it. I mean, I see you shaking your head when you're talking about it, and you're feeling good about it. Can you talk about that aspect? Like, you're telling people, it's a little autobiographical.

HAMMER: Yeah, the record deals directly from everybody's standpoint, not just from the "Hammer Man" standpoint. But from everybody's standpoint… *nobody can stop you from doing what you want to do or being what you want to be, no matter what comes in your way. In your mind, it's got to be all good.*

> Life Coach Lesson #2 (okay, I will stop)

BK: You're no stranger to positive messages. To me, that's as positive as it gets. Although with the heavy funk, you don't realize that you're coming off, you know what I'm saying?

HAMMER: Exactly, exactly right. Well, because it's not meant to be a message in terms of social commentary.

It's not what it's about, this is more of a message in terms of an individual thing, more of a street message. It's more, you know, from the standpoint of the way we come at each other on the streets, but it's a verbal assault, you know, it's a verbal assault.

BK: Yeah, you're like a captain there. What about as far as the actual title, "It's All Good?" Um, to me, it's one of the things that probably just came about when you're just saying "hey, it's all good" you know? How did it come about?

HAMMER: It's a term that we use in Oakland, you know, in the Bay Area, in the Big Bad Bay, we use it a lot… it's just a common phrase, you know, we say, "Man, how you feeling? Oh, it's all good." You know, it means everything is cool. You know, it's all good.

BK: What about as far as Funky Headhunter?

HAMMER: Well, the whole phrase "Funky Headhunter" is dealing with the music. Headhunter is the mission, you know? I'm out to get to the heads of my competitors who, you know, have risen they head up in the past, you know, to say anything against the Hammer Man. Hey, I'm coming to get your head.

BK: Okay now, which brings me to—I followed your career for a while now, you would figure that someone in your position, you wouldn't even say that you've done it, you've been there…

HAMMER: Oh yeah but nevertheless, there comes a time you know, when because I've done it all, this was a good motivating factor for me. It's like, hey, "what do you have to say about this?" Or there's always the interviews, they ask me questions about things that somebody has said that they may have read or saw on television or whatever the case is, heard on the radio. And they asked me those questions. So you don't have to ask me now. Because on the "Funky Headhunter," I addressed it. I addressed it because it's something that I've wanted to do, but just didn't get around to it until now.

> See how Hammer says "they" about the interviewers trying to create something out of nothing? And this is before social media negativity, clickbait and likes. But my takeaway is that he didn't lump me in with the others. We are just chatting like two old friends, one a superstar and the other a rapper setting the record straight. I kid.

BK: What about you? Every time an artist goes into a new album, they have a certain, not necessarily an agenda, but there's something specific they want to get across. It seems like you had a little bit of a mission. Was there something when you sat down to make this record? Because I don't know if you actually had a label at the time. I mean, what was going on?

HAMMER: Oh no…I've always had a label, there's never been a period or a point when I didn't have a label. The only time that I didn't have a label was when Capitol Records and myself decided that we weren't going to come to terms and we agreed to disagree. And at that point, I decided that I would make my home somewhere else. So it was up to me, of the many various labels that wanted to sign me, where I wanted to go. And I ended up with the place, understanding that a Hammer being available on the market is a very expensive entity, and not everybody can afford to come to the table. You know, it costs a lot of money to sign a Hammer. Anytime you sell, you know, millions and millions of records—and your last album sold over five million copies—it's very, you know, it's not a big market because everybody can't afford you. So once I narrowed it down to the labels that could afford me, and where I thought I might be comfortable, then I kind of zoomed in on the ones that had the right staff, and I felt were headed in the same direction as me.

BK: Azoff.

HAMMER: And that ended up being Cassandra Mills in Irving Azoff's office at Giant Records, you know, they had the right game plan. And, you know, they understand exactly where the Hammer Man is headed and so it was a perfect marriage.

> Did I ever tell you my personal Irving Azoff story? It's a good one. It involves the industry titan's wife and the group Color Me Badd. Nothing salacious, just hilarious. Maybe the next book.

BK: Does all this stuff, because you have your head involved in the business aspect as well of your career, does it affect the music when you're dealing with all these disturbances on the outside?

HAMMER: Not at all, no. Music is separate. Music is a whole different world, you know, the creative is separate from the business. But when I'm in there doing my music, I deal with the issues or the subject matter that, you know, I want to deal with on songs. And it's a lot different than dealing with business in a different form. But nevertheless, at some point they come together, but not on the record. They don't.

BK: What about as far as the fact that this album, after you sell like five million records, and then before that, like 10 million, what about the pressure level for you to produce the goods?

HAMMER: No pressure. Oh, it's no pressure.

BK: How do you keep that away?

HAMMER: Because I make music and when I make music, it's out of my hands once I create the product. And you know, giving it my all, I give it out to the public to enjoy it.

> Preach! Lesson for the creatives. Sometimes you just got to go with your gut, believe in your talent, and put your "art" out as YOU feel and let the market decide. Easier said than done, but if you're trying to manufacture or curate to what "you" think will sell, it's not gonna work. Authenticity was the key in the '90s, and it still rings true today.

BK: Is it difficult to constantly, in a sense, try and not necessarily outdo, but just to put the best stuff to maintain to prove yourself? Especially as we know, there's a lot of people that love to knock down their heroes.

HAMMER: Well, you have to be able to deal with that, you know, there's good and bad that come with success and you just have to be able to deal with both sides. But I'm not a new artist. I've been doing this for seven years, successfully. And I know the media very well, I have an education with the media that goes all the way back to 1991. I mean, I should say 1971, when I was a bat boy with the Oakland A's as a little kid. So I've watched the ballplayers and athletes, you know, they deal with the press for 20 years now, you know, so it was expected. And anytime you rise to the level of success that the Hammer has, and has maintained that level, there will always be people in the media who will look to try to pull you down. But they can't do that, you know, so they can make, they can write things on, you know, untruths, and they can say things, they can't change reality.

> Life Coach Lesson #3: Watch and learn. As a 9-year-old bat boy working for the Oakland A's, Hammer had a front row seat to superstar Reggie Jackson's combative relationship with the media. I don't think I knew at the time of this interview that Reggie was rumored to have given Stanley Kirk Burrell the "Hammer" nickname, but here was a missed opportunity to get it on record at the time. Instead, I decided to go with the lighter side and ask about his single.

BK: Let's talk about "Pumps in a Bump." I mean, that's a fun video. It's a fun song. Can you talk to me how that came about? I have a feeling about how it came about, but I'd rather hear it from you.

HAMMER: Well, "Pumps in a Bump" was just a big party, you know? It was a pool party at my house with a lot of my friends. And the song was my reminder to women that it's pretty cool you know, that a lot of women today wear the baggy clothes that a lot of the men wear and everything. But don't forget the fact that we still think you look lovely and beautiful when you throw on those fierce pair of pumps and have that sexy, sexy, sexy derriere shaking. We love all that. So you know, it's like, we love the women with the pumps and the bumps, it's not a put down, it's a lift up you know? We're saying we were praising women, we love them, when, you know, seeing a woman walking down the street with those sexy pumps on.

BK: I actually saw the video. God, it'd be great to be friends with the Hammer.

HAMMER: [laughs] Yeah, we have nice, we have nice parties up there.

> That was my lame attempt at angling for an invite to a Hammer pool party. Never happened, although I did attend a P Diddy party in Las Vegas. There was no "freak off," but I digress. Back to Hammer. We then talked about some of his side ventures, but didn't get into the pressures or stories about his reported financial difficulties. We kept it light, but he did offer up something I believe to be super important (and so did he).

BK: The one thing that I liked most about you throughout this whole time when people were naysaying and all that stuff is that you put a lot of people to work.

HAMMER: Oh, yeah, I've had the opportunity to employ, you know—and I say this opportunity, because it's because of my success—I've been able to employ like, up to 150 African Americans from my community for, you know, four or five years. And that's one of the things that I enjoy doing is giving back to my community so that we create, you know, stronger economic basis, throughout our community.

BK: See you notice I am still sticking on the positive side. Another positive effect, and it's the one that cannot be denied is that there's a lot of kids out there, still want to be rappers, or positive because of you. Do you have time to either sit back and just actually realize that or do you need people like myself to tell you that that's happened?

HAMMER: I appreciate people like yourself telling me but I'm out there, you know, so the kids come up to me, you know, so I see them all the time, in different situations. Basketball games, football games, you know, different places where they see the Hammer Man, you know, they come up to me, ask for autographs. And you know, say "Hey man… I dance just like you" and you know, "I'm gonna be like you." So, the kids are very open and because I'm a person who really gets out there a lot, I'm able to hear it from the kids themselves directly. So, I appreciate it.

> Side note story about kids…when I was interviewing Maurice White of Earth, Wind & Fire (did I drop something), we were talking about MC Hammer because the EWF legend asked him to rap on their 1990 single "Wanna Be The Man." How it happened ties into this conversation. Maurice's 12-year-old son was a HUGE fan of the MC and kept playing his records for his father. And in a twist of creative fate, Earth, Wind & Fire ended up being on the same plane as MC Hammer's band. Introductions were made, and a record came about. But it would never have happened if Hammer wasn't a positive role model as Maurice explained to me in our interview in August of 1990.

EARTH, WIND & FIRE'S MAURICE WHITE: Well, my main reason for bringing him into the fold relative to the song "Wanna Be The Man" is his positive image that he has on kids. That was my main thrust. You know, it's like if I'm gonna be associated with somebody, I want to be associated with someone who's making a positive contribution to the kids. And who, you know, who better than MC Hammer?

> Back to MC Hammer, Hammer Man, Funky Headhunter, aka Stanley.

BK: Last question is basically just looking back, because your career just kind of took off. It went so high, you can't get higher than that. Looking back, you can look back on it now because it's been a few years. I mean, were you caught up in it, like how was it to be on that high where everything was just going right nonstop?

HAMMER: Well, you know, it exploded from day one. Let's see, because my first album, again, was a platinum plus album, which for at that time, rap wasn't really, not too many rappers was selling a million records. My very first album, you know, almost sold two million copies. And it was up here along the way. So, I was just kind of riding on out, you know, and it continued, it continues to ride, you know, at a very high pace, and very fast face, you know, life in the music business moves very quickly. Fortunately, I've had the staying power.

> Hammer was an important fixture in pop music and culture through the '90s with his unique style (pants), dancing, and infectious hit records. It's interesting that I didn't bring up his biggest anthem, "Can't Touch This." I forget why, but there had to be a reason I didn't ask or get a story. Fortunately, I am able to pull an anecdote from the Super Freak himself, Rick James who I interviewed in October of 1997. I made light of the fact that MC Hammer's use of his single may have paid for a few houses and that was all he needed to set him off.

RICK JAMES: Yeah, you know, it made millions of dollars. I mean, it's a joke, but it's true. But if it was up to me, Hammer wouldn't have recorded it... me and James Brown, were talking about it, you know, it's like, we would hear rap records that we couldn't play for our kids. And we wasn't with that. And James said, well look, you know, "I'm not gonna let them use no more of my stuff. I don't know how you feel about it." And I said, well, "I'm gonna go, I'm going in your direction." So me and James really said to hell with it, you know, we had enough money. We had millions of dollars sitting in the bank, it wasn't like, we're gonna go broke if rappers didn't record us or something. And, unless they're gonna say something that's not derogatory, and it's not demeaning the Black race or demeaning the Black woman. And that's what we're coming from. And to this day, I still come from that place. And so I told my people, I didn't want any more rappers doing my stuff. And they said, "okay Rick," you know, because all this money was coming in from these different rappers. I said I didn't approve this... and they said but we did, and I said well no more, just no more. End it [chuckles].

> So now you have the backstory, bring it home.

RICK JAMES: And I was driving in California one day, and this record comes on. And then it's like, top 10 in the pop charts or something. And it starts off, and I hear "Super Freak" and I think, uh, here's my record out again, great, you know, I said whoa they bringing me back. Fantastic. And then hear the break in it say, "you can't touch this." And then it goes on. And then he says "me and my music rock so hard," I say "me and my music?" And I just had enough. And I got on the phone and I start calling up. It was like, I don't know, maybe three in the morning here, two in the morning, I just left the club and I was on full, and a carload of women and I was really pissed off. And I called my accountants and business people back east. And I said, you know, I just heard this record, you know, just "you can't touch this" crap in it. And what is this? Didn't I tell you people I don't want any more rappers doing my stuff? And they said, "Rick, calm down, calm down, you're gonna make so many millions of dollars in the next six months." I said, "okay, never mind." So that's how that went, you know, and, and basically, it wasn't harmful. Hammer did not make a harmful record. I mean lyrically wise, I mean, any kid can listen to that record and enjoy it.

And every adult too. Lessons learned. MC Hammer's positivity was a green light to legends like Maurice White and Rick James, as well as future generations of artists. He was an original and I hope up and coming artists follow his creative lead and positive role in the community, and NOT purchase racehorses or other businesses that might send you into bankruptcy. I kid of course, but you can't deny that this Hammer Man has had one colorful life. And for this conversation, the Bay Area legend made an impact on me as a young journalist and revisiting this chapter of my life has already influenced my current thinking. Please Hammer Don't Hurt 'em.

WHAT CAN I SAY ABOUT AALIYAH? Well, first of all, how do you actually pronounce her name properly? To this day, I still don't get it right and that's literally the first question I ever asked her?!?! And she told me!

Aaliyah is no longer with us, as she was tragically killed in an airplane accident in the Bahamas in 2001 at the age of 22. I remember being sad, and every time I would hear one of her songs or see her in a movie, there was a sense of loss to me, too young.

Age is a theme in this interview as she recorded her debut album *Age Ain't Nothing But A Number* when she was 14 years old and I met her when she was promoting it at the tender age of 15. Her debut single "Back & Forth" was already climbing the charts (one of my favorites tracks to this day), and when I initially listened to the album, I thought her voice was velvety pure, silky smooth…not young. She had a maturity about her.

But what strikes me to this day is how much of a legacy she left in such a short life span of music. Kids these days and some of my contemporaries think that she had a major impact on music but as you'll find out from this conversation, she literally gives most of the initial credit to Robert Kelly.

Yes, R. Kelly.

It was early May of 1994, I made the trip to 9000 Sunset Boulevard, entered the offices of Zomba Records, and set up my tape recorder in a conference room and hit record. I hadn't listened back to this interview since her death, but I knew we had a special conversation. I always joke "too soon" on everything, but for this project the time has come to press play.

BK: 123 test 123 Aaliyah interview or Aaliyah interview, we'll find out in a second, 5-5-94 at Zomba on 9000 Sunset.

> A bubbly Aaliyah enters, I attach a microphone to her lapel.

BK: Hi, Hi. Hi. Hi. Who are you? What's your name again?

AALIYAH: Aaliyah.

BK: I'm just making sure.

AALIYAH: Okay, Aaliyah.

BK: You never know it might have changed.

[Aaliyah laughs]

AALIYAH: All right. No, it's Michael Jackson now.

BK: Oh Michael, wow you look a little different Michael. [Aaliyah laughs] All right, well, so I just want to start off by saying congratulations.

AALIYAH: Oh, thank you very much.

BK: You know, I do this thing for a living, been watching the charts. I see your name, I'm like who the hell…[Aaliyah laughs] What's this all about? Your feelings on what's going on?

AALIYAH: How the single's going? Yeah. Well, it's amazing because my manager calls me, which is also my uncle.

> Her uncle was Barry Hankerson, and while we shared the same first name, we also shared a mutual love for Gladys Knight—me as a fan, and him as one of her ex-husbands.

AALIYAH: He'll call me and tell me that it's, you know, number three on Billboard, and number 22 on pop, R&B is three and pop is 22. And he's saying how great that is for the single and I'm like, I'm very excited. And he's like, you should be more excited, you should be jumping around and everything. But I'm not the type of person to really jump around and be happy but I'm very excited because I know this is unusual. But I'm really glad everyone liked it.

BK: Can you talk about the story behind it, maybe what it's about?

AALIYAH: Okay, well me and Robert, one night, we were in studio. And we were working on some other songs. And we were dancing and everything and we kind of did this little dance that's in the video. And he said, "hey, that's a nice, nice, cute little dance." He said "back and forth." And so then he

BK: kind of thought of a song. That's really where it came from, the dance. That's why we use it in the video.

BK: What about this fact, I mean, you're a new artist, you're young. Was there anything specific that you wanted to get on? You know, hey, this is my first record... I gotta have something like this on it, was it anything like that?

AALIYAH: No, not really, *Robert kind of took control and did the whole album and I listened to him because I guess you could say he kind of raised me musically. Because the talent was there. I knew what I wanted to do. But as far as experience, he'd been out there longer. And he showed me, you know, what to do as far as music, image wise and everything. So really, I'm like his baby.* [Aaliyah chuckles] So I really didn't have anything to say "well I want to put this in there." I'll probably come around later on when I get used to this.

> She did chuckle...

BK: Well, since you mentioned Robert's name a couple of times, I know who you're talking about. I've interviewed the man. [Aaliyah laughs] Yeah, yeah, I did. He is definitely a lot of fun, very cool cat. Talk about who we're talking about. I mean, this album was written and produced by Robert Kelly, R. Kelly for producers who don't know. Can you talk about that aspect who you know, who it was written by and produced?

AALIYAH: Mr. R. Kelly, Robert Kelly wrote and produced the whole album, everything.

BK: Everything.

AALIYAH: Every little thing.

BK: But he also did it specially for you in a way, can you talk about that?

AALIYAH: Yeah, well, I guess because I…me and him are really close. I've known him for three years now. So it's like, I guess he put his little special things in there for me. It wasn't just like, I have to do this song, do it and it's over with because we know outside of the studio, we're friends. So that's probably why you know, people say especially for Aaliyah.

> R. Kelly is around 27, and Aaliyah is around 15, but plenty of young singers work with seasoned producers. But, if she's known him for 3 years already, that means she was dancing back and forth with him when she was 13 or 14. I know, "Age Ain't Nothing But A Number."

BK: You know, a lot of the songs deal with relationships, fun, you know, very positive, right? Was that just the vibe between the "he knows that that's what you would like," how did that workout?

AALIYAH: Well, we've talked about like some of the things that would go on the album and our you know, my feelings on it. And he got that vibe from me because like he never writes things down on paper. His songs just kind of go off the top of his head. And he'll tell me what to sing. And then I'll sing it, so I guess he got the vibe really.

BK: Since we're talking a little bit about the studio,

what is he like? What is R Kelly like? I mean, I know what he's like. But from your take…

AALIYAH: He's sensitive, caring, and if he hears this, he's gonna be like, "Well, I lift weights." He's a very fun-loving person. And it's been great working with him. [Aaliyah does her church lady impression and says] "Well, isn't that something, that's so cute." He's a very sweet person, and he's sensitive to people's needs. And he listened to me like if I did have something to say…if I said, "let's put this in," he probably would have considered it. But I really listened to him on this one. It's been great working with him. I learned a lot as far as writing, producing all of that. It's been great.

BK: Well, since we're talking about being in the studio, what was it like in the studio? I read through some of the production notes talking about the fact that I know how R. Kelly is in the studio. But you even mentioned, you're a little bit of a perfectionist.

AALIYAH: Ugh, we're both perfectionists. We'll go over a line a million times to get it just right. I mean, even if it sounds like it's right, it's not. We will go over again until it is perfect. And that happens a lot. Oh boy, he made me sing it one more time. Just do one more time. And it's like, it's tiring. But you know it works out in the end.

BK: Let's talk about the title of the album. I know it's also a song and will probably be released as a single as well. Age Ain't Nothing But A Numbah!

AALIYAH: Right right [laughs]. Well that title just speaks for itself, age ain't nothing but a number. People asking me, how old are you, what 15, 14? And I'll say "age ain't nothing but a number," the title of the album because I feel that people should just…take this album for what it is and not really be concerned about my age. It's not just a kiddie album, it's not an adult album, everyone can relate. And that's why I say age, you know, don't worry about.

BK: Well, I'm not like other journalists. So how old are you?

AALIYAH: [laughs loud] Okay. Well, "age ain't nothing but a number."

BK: That's a catchy phrase, you should put like a song or something, you know.

AALIYAH: You know what, we might, that's an idea. Thanks.

BK: I should listen to the record huh?

AALIYAH: Yeah.

BK: Well, you know, since you bring up that, I mean, you don't look a day over 35. I mean, how are you about 30?

AALIYAH: About 40? Really.

BK: Hey, what about a younger guy liking an older girl?

AALIYAH: Same…it's all around for everyone really.

BK: So if there's like the 12-year-old out there going, oh, well Aaliyah she's…

AALIYAH: [laughing] That's happening.

BK: And his friends are like what are you talking about, and he's like "age ain't nothing but a number."

AALIYAH: Uh huh, that song is a really good little phrase.

BK: Now we'll just talk a little bit about you. Where are you from?

AALIYAH: I was born in Brooklyn, New York. And we moved to Detroit when I was a baby.

Around two or three, we moved to Detroit. And that's where I was raised. And that's it.

> I was born in Brooklyn too, college outside of Detroit! See, we're very similar except for the music talent.

BK: Good childhood? What was childhood like?

AALIYAH: Well, ever since I was little and I started going to school, it's been music, really, because I've been in like all the school plays from elementary school. I was in 42nd Street, like a lot of Broadway musicals. And I sang at various functions around the Michigan area, you know, of course, including Detroit, and I've been singing ever since then. I mean, my mother we would sing constantly cause she can also sing. And my parents helped me a lot. You know, I had a vocal, I have a vocal trainer. I still got her, Wendy Petty, and I take piano lessons. And now I go to a performing arts high school. So it's like, every day of my life has always been something dealing with music. Always.

BK: You go to the Detroit school of performing (arts) right now. It's gonna be kind of odd. Like, you're still there! I mean, it is a performing arts high school, right? I mean, how did you get into that? You have to audition?

AALIYAH: You had to have a portfolio and you had to go and audition to what major you wanted to be in, which was vocal. And I had to do two songs, one in a foreign language and another one. Anyway, they accepted me.

BK: Okay, so since you said, I gotta ask. What songs did you sing and did you nail it and what was it like?

AALIYAH: Yes I nailed it. I sang "Ava Maria" in Latin, and I sang "The Star-Spangled Banner" and they accepted me. I got a call right after auditions and said I made it to the school.

BK: When you grew up in Detroit, it's almost like, everybody knows this is our city. This is our music, the heritage. Can you talk about you know, growing up? Did you listen to the Motown sound? What did you listen to growing up?

AALIYAH: Growing up I listened to Aretha, Diana, my mom loved her. And who else was it? That's really about it. And Smokey. Yeah. And my mother was in love with him. So we listened to him. And you know, I listen to a lot of different types of music, though, because my brother likes opera and everything. So I'm really open to all types of music. He loves classical music, and I listen to Luther, Billie Holiday, everybody growing up.

BK: Yeah, I noticed the operatic influences on the record. You know, every once in a while, you get that?

> This is BK sarcasm 101. Class in session.

BK: So, since you mentioned your families, let's talk about your family. What's it like?

AALIYAH: We're really happy and they're happy for me, very happy because we've been working for this for a long,

long time. You know, they've been pushing me, they've been behind me 100%. And they've been there for me from the beginning. My brother, my mom and my dad has been, it's been great. And they're very, very happy for me.

> Wowza...talk about things going well, world is your oyster type vibe. I was so used to hearing about the hardships and struggles for one's ART, it felt good to hear from a well-adjusted kid with a supportive family, not to mention blessed with talent for days! Listening back to the audio this many years later, it hurts even more that her life was taken so tragically, so early.

BK: It's a beautiful name, where does it come from? What does it mean?

AALIYAH: Aaliyah? Aaliyah is Arabic Muslim, and it means the highest most exalted one, the best.

BK: Wow, that's a lot to live up to. You know.

AALIYAH: I know it is. Have to say yes, it's hard. It's hard to live up to that, but I want to, so I'm gonna do it. Gonna do it.

BK: It's really nice to meet someone like yourself. Quote unquote, a little younger than most, yet, still has that positive attitude. You know, it's really, it's a pleasure. I've interviewed a lot of people and it's really nice to see that.

And after revisiting this interview, I echo my quick summation at the time which was that it was really nice to meet her, and this conversation was a pleasure!

She definitely made a lasting mark in the music world, in pop culture. It's tough to include her future plans in this transcript as her dreams were cut short. But she told me she wanted her debut album to go platinum, make that triple platinum (three million copies sold). She doubled that and then some... Check! She wanted to act in movies, she was awesome as the lead in 2001's hit film *Romeo Must Die*. Check! I can say that as "technically" I am a movie critic. Actress, check!

There are a few lessons here for me... when I hear Billy Joel sing "Only The Good Die Young," obviously it's not necessarily true. It does seem like a lot of assholes live to be old. So my takeaway is that there's a lot of true artists and friends of mine whose lives have been cut short, but have made a true impact on me. And I need to reflect on their influences, pay some personal homage to them. Recognize the past, but look to the future with another nugget of knowledge in my noggin. Also, there are no guarantees in life. So live it.

> One addendum. At the end of the interview, I gave Aaliyah the chance to be a guest DJ on one of our syndicated radio shows. It's a very simple "promo" or "liner" as we call it, but it gives an artist an opportunity to shout out another artist. She chose two...can you guess one of them? Hint: it rhymes with R. Kelly.

AALIYAH: Hey, what's up? This is Aaliyah and I'm taking over as the weekly guest DJ. I'm gonna play some R. Kelly for you because hey, this is my number one homie.

> The second one was Jodeci as they were hitting on all cylinders in 1994.

AALIYAH: Hey, this is Aaliyah and I'm taking over as the weekly guest DJ. Right now I'm going to play some Jodeci for you because hey, they're all that!

> So true, Jodeci almost made it into this edition of Classic Conversations, as I had several with them including a special one for their debut album. To quote the highest most exalted one, "they're all that."

In honor of Aaliyah singing Oleta Adam's "Get Here" for her audition with R. Kelly, I included the publicity still with Oleta. Maybe I included it because she said it was "such a joy" meeting me.

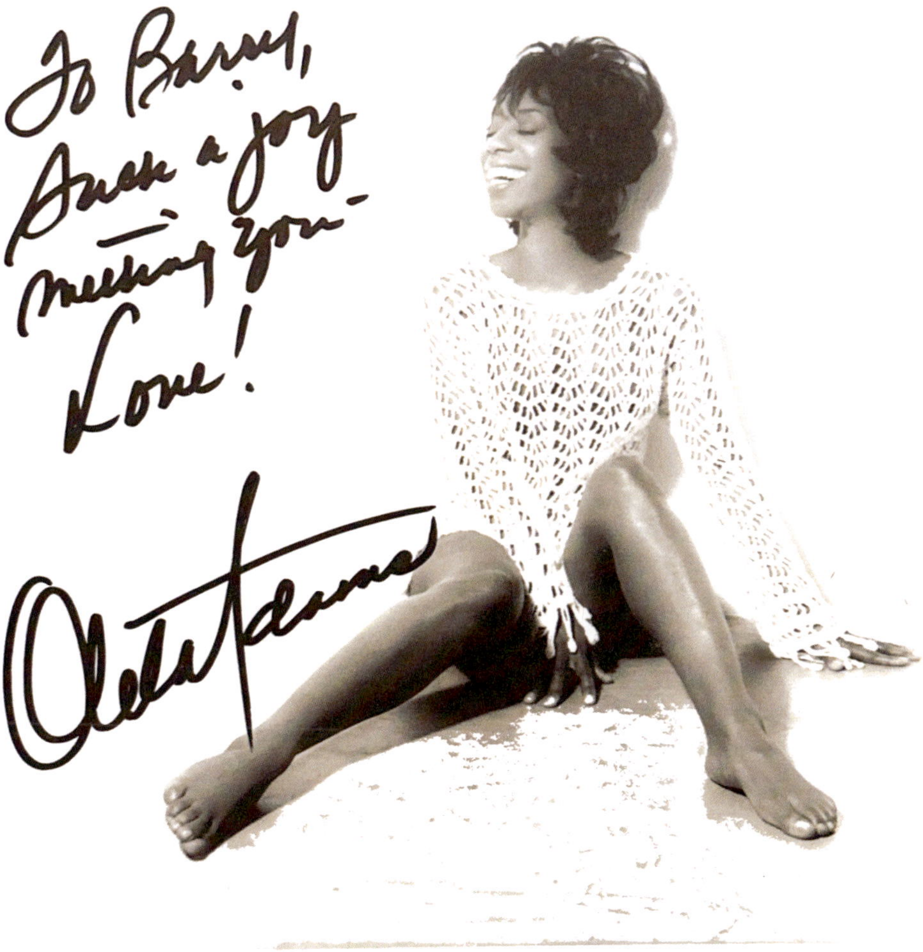

OLETA ADAMS

fontana

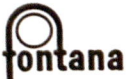

LUTHER DAY 2/16/05

:29
1:30 Awards 12/4/96 → "In terms of the business.... I love the events, 4
2:24 Grew up a Motown Child
3:24 on "Love The One You're With"
7:00 Response of Fans to SONGS, the LP
7:37 *quote used → a- "I'm tired of groundwork now, I've been making LPs for 15... we'll get."
  (12 secs)
9:40 → on "Love The One You're With"
10:50 on "Endless Love"
12:05 on "Always And Forever"
13:10 Ten consecutive LPs → "8/14/98" "I am Gonzalez? understand the research.... That's a cool distinction.
14:?? on how he does it → ethic, vision, sight CD ahead (used) → Vibe 12/11/97 "I think its... CD unheard."
15:17 on keeping it fresh → no ego hangs, 10/8/96 "I mean we could... they're well executed."
  Vibe 7/10/98 "I was never prone... music & your career.
  The saw big artists go though problems and never get ungluded 6/4/96 "I saw them go through... your career, which both of them were."
  (Roberta Flack → Anita Baker)
16:10 Vibe A perfectionist - won't stop 'til it's right.... Vibe 1/23/98 "I'm a perfectionist... do differently."
  People try to under what it is that you do...
  on being a
  Pop Artist → admires crossover success... long, enduring and fabulous
  declines to describe his music... he's not making science
  (lets people (he's not saving lives)) used 6/25
  → it's sugar? things that they a/... → I most enjoy leisure... rules of thumb
    Vibe 8/11/98 "I always decline rules of thumb
  he's a romantic, it's like a/a movie... love is the underscoring theme...

MY HANDWRITTEN NOTES FROM THE CONVERSATION—A GLIMPSE INTO THE PREP WORK UTILIZING THE INTERVIEW SOUNDBITES.

I REMEMBER FEELING AMPED TO MEET LUTHER VANDROSS—obviously for his legendary status, but also because I knew about his unique journey. From jingles singer to background vocalist, to one-name icon, Luther's path to stardom was a masterclass in persistence. Long before the term "10,000 hours" became a mantra, Luther was living it. He was a writer, producer, and performer—a true pioneer in the game.

I was set to interview him for the release of *Songs*, his cover album featuring classics like Crosby, Stills & Nash's "Love the One You're With" (which he transformed into a gospel revival) and the timeless Lionel Richie/Diana Ross ballad "Endless Love," where he enlisted Mariah Carey for their own legendary duet.

But instead of the typical hotel or record label office, Luther invited me to his Beverly Hills home for the interview. And yes, his crib was everything I imagined it would be—stylish, elegant, and effortlessly cool. Now, I was doing the interview for radio, so I needed a quiet space, but there was some construction going on at the time. We literally had to move around his house a few times before we finally settled into his sunken living room, complete with shag carpeting and a wet bar. The vibe? Pure Luther.

And let me tell you, Luther did not disappoint. He dropped some serious knowledge, on everything from the realities of fame to the importance of staying grounded in an industry that's anything but stable.

I've heard countless artists say there's no playbook for what happens when you skyrocket to fame—no class or manual to guide you once you're thrust into the spotlight. This theme comes up often in my interviews with artists who reached stardom but still had to navigate the chaos on their own. But Luther? He had a unique perspective. Having seen stardom from both sides—behind the scenes, behind the star, and then on the stage himself—his insights were pure gold. He stayed grounded, he navigated the madness. He told me his story.

There is only one Luther… well, that statement gets debunked in the mic check…

BK: Test 123, Test 123 interview with Luther Vandross. I just want to make sure I'm here with Luther Vandross.

LUTHER: Test test.

BK: You are testing perfectly. You know, Mr. Luther Ronzoni Vandross, and don't think I don't know that. What is up with that? I'm getting hungry already.

LUTHER: Yeah, Ronzoni's my middle name. When my mother had me, my father's name was Luther. And they asked my mother, they said, "Do you have a middle name for the baby?" And she was, you know, all disoriented, you know? And she looked on the little nightstand next to the bed and there was this ad for spaghetti that said, "Ronzoni Sono Buoni, Ronzoni is so good." And she says, "Yeah, okay, okay, Ronzoni."

BK: THAT is NOT a true story!

LUTHER: That is absolutely a true story. You could call her up now and ask her. When you call my house, they don't call me Luther. They call me Ronnie. That's why my publishing company is called Uncle Ronnie's music company. Ronnie is a derivative of Ronzoni, which is my name.

> Could be the best mic check level question and answer I've ever heard. Okay, so onto the interview.

BK: Let's talk about the album as a whole, what has been the response? What's been the response from some of the artists that you've decided to cover… to remake. Not to remake, reinvent.

LUTHER: It's been very positive, those who I have heard from. Lionel Richie sent me a message about loving it. Someone who works in his house said that all day long, he had the album on a loop. He just played it over and over and over you know? That made my day. I mean, that was great. Barbra Streisand sent me a lovely message that she loved "Evergreen." Dionne Warwick called me about "What The World Needs Now is Love" and Burt Bacharach called. Who else, Roberta Flack. Roberta did a PSA public service announcement for me, and she had them play the song over and over "Killing Me Softly." She just really loved it. So it's been really positive.

BK: I had it looping in my office.

LUTHER: Oh, good. They told me your office was the phone booth down on the corner of Fairfax. [laughs]

BK: It's looping in there, if you drive by you'll hear it.

> I love this man! He's got a sense of humor, and he was busting my balls right away.

BK: There was an interesting quote in the press notes saying, and it's from you saying that, you know, "sure I've done records, but for some reason, everything still feels new." How do you keep it fresh?

LUTHER: Well, see, I was never prone to big, big, humongous ego bouts anyway, you know. I wasn't raised like that and some of my favorite people who I got to work with as a background singer before I became a solo artist, I saw them go through the paces of their careers. I saw Roberta Flack in emergencies when the cases didn't show up, or whatever. I worked with David Bowie—and he had major, major productions—and I never saw him become unglued about anything, you know, and that was an example for me. Oh, so you can be very, very famous and successful and still civil and sober about your whole approach to your music and your career? Which both of them were, so those were examples for me. And, you know, I'm a perfectionist, that I really am. And I don't stop until it's right. And that's worked out to be a good quality for me.

BK: If anyone who knows a little bit about your resume from where you started, and who you were singing with on your way up, in essence, seems natural, that you are a mainstream artist.

LUTHER: Oh, yeah, it's long overdue. See, I was never some esoteric type of singer, who appealed only to a small corner of the population. This is the same voice that sang Pepsi Cola, Juicy Fruit, GE, AT&T, NBC, you know, Miller beer. All of this is the same voice that brought all of that to you. So it's not some sort of esoteric approach, you know, "Never Too Much," and records like "Stop to Love" and "Give Me the Reason." You know, those are all records that peaked in the 50s you know. And yeah, I mean, and who is that a reflection on? I think I sang 'em fine.

> Luther is alluding to the fact that these hit songs that we all know, never crossed to the pop charts. But he's not angry. Lessons...

LUTHER: But what I'm saying to you is that I get asked a lot now about the pop category, you know, about how I feel about that. And the point is I feel great, but I also feel that it's overdue. I didn't change anything. I didn't go out and buy a bunch of blonde wigs and take an album cover, you know, with a blonde for the cover of the *Songs* album. I didn't do anything different, it's still Luther.

BK: It's fortunate because one time I remember you coming back(stage), maybe it might have been Soul Train Awards, was probably the AMAs or something. And I was a little kid, I asked you, I said, "I know you did some background sessions, name names." You said, "oh I don't know." I'm like "name names" because I felt like no one else knew.

LUTHER: Uh huh. Well thanks…

BK: Can you brag just a little bit like, you know, who you, who you might have…

LUTHER: Sang background for before my first solo record?

BK: Before the break.

LUTHER: Oh, yeah. Well, it all started with David Bowie. David was absolutely the one. David used to…I used to sing. We used to go up to David's room to play records. And I would just sing because he'd always have a big suite and it'd be a piano or something. And he said, you know, he says, "YOU have got IT, whatever that IT is, you got IT. You know, you're gonna make it Luther." That kind of encouragement. He introduced me to Bette (Midler), introduced me to Arif Mardin. Arif Mardin is a well renowned, well credentialed producer. For Arif, I sang background for Chaka Khan, for Carly Simon, for Ringo Starr. I went on tour with Todd Rundgren, I sang with The J. Geils Band and I was the original member of Chic. I was the one [sings] "Freak Out," yeah, those are those records. And then Roberta Flack and Quincy Jones. And I mean, the list goes on and on. And Roberta was the one who encouraged me to pursue a solo career.

BK: I love that. And then when she says to you, "you're solo, you ain't singing backup for me."

LUTHER: Yeah. She said "as much as I would love to have you sit on that stool and continue to sing 'ooh, and ah' for me, I really think that you ought to go and pursue your own solo career. You deserve it." And I took her advice.

BK: It's kind of nice when you have people like David Bowie or Roberta Flack saying you have IT.

LUTHER: Yeah. It is.

BK: Give a little bit more of a confidence boost or did you know you had IT?

LUTHER: I knew I loved IT, whatever IT was. Having IT, I was too young in my career to know whether or not I had IT. See, I wasn't good at being my own cheerleader you know. I needed that external push and vote of confidence in order to make me feel, you know, worth it.

> Honest lessons…

BK: Another thing that I didn't know until about—let's say, five, six years ago—is when I started getting into music and writing about it, I didn't realize how much of a songwriter you were even from back in the day, even the beginning. When did you first get interested in writing songs?

LUTHER: Well, the first song that I ever had out, this is such an interesting story. I was on the road with David Bowie in '74. But in 1972, I had met some independent producers who had met a Broadway producer who had a vision to do a play. He said, I'm going to do an all Black version of *The Wizard of Oz*. And…we're taking each of the scenes, and we're writing all new songs for them. And I submitted for four different scenes, four songs and that was that. And in 1974, I went on the road with David. And in the latter part of the tour, he says, "oh I can't wait to get to New York next week." And we all said, "well, why?" He says, "I'm going to Broadway, I'm going to see an all Black version of *The Wizard of Oz*." And something in my mind went ding, ding, ding, ding. And I said, wow, I said, "many years ago, I wrote a song for a similar idea. I wonder if it has anything to do with anything." Come to find out, my mother and I had moved, and they didn't have a forwarding number. And they totally were glad to find me. There was all of this royalty and residual stuff, you know, to be collected. And the play was on Broadway. And it was a big smash starring Stephanie Mills.

> The song was "Everybody Rejoice." It was later featured in the 1978 film version of *The Wiz*, sung by cast members Diana Ross, Michael Jackson, Nipsey Russell, and Ted Ross (aka *The Wiz* Stars). Yes, an interesting story.

BK: Talk to me about producing these days. I mean, what do you get from producing, what is it like?

LUTHER: In the beginning when I was younger, I felt that I needed to do it all. I felt that I had something to prove and something to show and I wanted to do it all. You know as time went on, I started enlisting co-producers to work with me to have the chance to leave the studio and know that the work would be continued. And it was an insurance, producing for me as an insurance policy that the vision and the final product agree. You know, otherwise, it gets way out of hand. You know, I love it. I love it in certain ways. It's like being a doctor, you know, you do an operation a certain way on Thursday, you find out that they discovered this little tube that if you inserted a certain way, you don't have to spend as many hours in the operating room. It's always ever-changing. There's always a new piece of equipment, there's always a new echo chamber, there's always new…I produce for the sake of mainly ensuring that the quality of my music is correctly protected. And then there are some projects that are irresistible. You know, like when Whitney calls and says, "OOOOh, Luther I know you got time to do one song, come on, do one song," you know, like that. And I'll go and do one song. Or Aretha, the same thing or Dionne or whoever's asked, you know, and that's when it's fun. It's a lot of fun.

BK: Dr. Vandross.

LUTHER: [laughs] Dr. Lu.

BK: Dr. Lu Code Blue stat.

> He gets my humor.

BK: Yeah. I want to come back to writing because you are a writer. What do you get from writing? We just talked about what you got from producing.

LUTHER: From writing, I get a chance to vent a little bit. I write maybe 30% of the songs as autobiographical and 70% of the songs are just from what I mean, it's like a movie. You know, you went to see *Love Story*. You know, Ryan O'Neal experienced in order to cry, and understand what he's feeling. So the same thing with a song, like that counts. It's the ability to depict and touch your life with the story that I'm telling. That's why "Killing Me Softly," such a great song. Because you see someone on stage who's singing about things that you yourself have experienced. Best thing that can happen as a songwriter happened. One time, I had a song called "Don't Want to Be a Fool." It was the single after "Power of Love." And this woman came up to me, she says "Can I just take one second? You know, I just want to tell you this," you know, she says, "I had a boyfriend for 10 or 11 years, who beat the mess out of me. He beat me up for all that time." She said "I stayed because I thought nobody else wanted me." She said, "and I stayed, because I thought this is the best that I would be able to get." She said "'Don't Want to Be a Fool' came out and I heard the song and no, no, no, I listened to the song and something made me listen again. And then I began to hear the song. And you said 'each time around, I tell myself, it's the game of love, ignore the signs and risk it all in the name of love." She says, "I listened to that song and when you said 'I decided not to let nobody kill me again' and 'I'll say to the end, I won't be a fool ever again.'" She says "I left him from what I got from that song." And that's all you could ever expect to do as a songwriter.

BK: I just got the chills like major when you said that.

> I just got the chills again when I listened back to this conversation, this specific story. So if there's anyone out there that needs to leave a toxic relationship, friendship, job, whatever, you can do it. Download "Don't Wanna Be a Fool" and make it your anthem. Life can be rough, but there can also be help, and eventual goodness.

BK: Yeah. Alright, that's two topics, third topic is singing. We talked about producing.

LUTHER: [Luther sings high notes, then low notes] I mean, oooooh, which am I as a Platter, a baritone [laughs]. I'm Flip Wilson as a baritone. Right. Whatever.

> He's hilarious and clearly enjoying himself, but in between the laughs, Luther drops nuggets of wisdom and positive themes. You can tell he's aware of the impact his craft has had, but he shares it in a way that makes you root for him even more. He's had some major mentors along the way, yet he's managed to forge his own path, blending their influence with his unique vision. I'm catching him at a moment where he's far from a rookie, but still climbing toward legendary status. After all, you don't choose to cover songs by icons like Aretha Franklin and Barbra Streisand unless you believe you can bring IT, whatever IT is.

BK: What do you get from letting it go, from singing?

LUTHER: Um, of the three, the one nearest and dearest to my heart is the singing. There is no experience comparable to it being 2:30 a.m., all the musicians have left, most of the other studios are empty. It's just you and the engineer. You turn all the lights down. All of the cello tracks have been bounced and pitched and harmonized and whatever. And I say, I just want to go give this song, just a little try. I haven't sung all day and you start singing, you know, you just start and you say, [singing] "Long ago and oh so far away, I fell in..." And you can't stop. You can't stop. There's nothing, you have nothing to do with it. There's a thing that you are just involved in.

> Please get the audio book if there ever is one, to hear Luther sing "Superstar" to me, in his house, in his sunken living room with shag carpet and a wet bar, my chills are multiplying listening to the tape. He had me at "Long ago"...

BK: Thank you for picking that song to do.

LUTHER: Oh, that song is, that's the oh, that's the tearjerker. That's the *Steel Magnolias* of songs. That's the, it's just the killer. It's the *Ordinary People* of songs.

BK: When did you have an idea that, like—we're talking about your voice—but when did you have an idea that your own voice was as smooth as silk. And I can say that, I'm a writer.

LUTHER: Um, you know, I listen back to the early records and to the early early ones. And that's something that just became a preference of mine. You know, as the years went by, how they say you can catch more flies with honey than you can with vinegar you know? I took that on as a vocal approach and I said in order to convince someone, I don't have to hit them over the head with a gavel. I don't have to be gruff. I'll leave the gruff to Rod Stewart and Teddy Pendergrass, they can cover the gruff territory. I want to cover the sort of soothe you, the lay on a hammock in front of the, you know, near the ocean. That's what I wanted my voice to do. And the only reason you wake up is just because it's getting cold, because it's getting dark. You know, that's how I wanted my voice to affect people.

BK: We were talking earlier, you mentioned the names, you say Aretha, you say Dionne, Diana, you in a sense have been able to—I've read about this—I mean, you lived out one of your major dreams.

LUTHER: Oh yeah. I got to produce all three of my favorite favorite singers, Aretha, Diana Ross and Dionne Warwick.

BK: How does that happen? I mean, in a sense, and what does it do for you as a person? More so than an artist, you know?

LUTHER: You know, who you are and who you become is kind of a brick by brick process. It's a layering of things that happen to you and decisions that you make. And each thing was very separate from the other. I was doing an interview when "Never Too Much" was out in 1981 for Rolling Stone magazine. And the last question was, well, now that you have a gold album, what could you want next? And my quote was, "I'd wrestle Bruno Sammartino for a chance to produce Aretha Franklin." And so about a month went by, and the phones rang. And I said "Hello?" And a woman's voice said "Vandross." And I mean, in those two syllables, I knew exactly who it was, my blood pressure must have gone up to two billion, over three billion. And the bottom numbers supposed to be smaller [chuckles]. She says "So when's the big match with Bruno?" I can't believe this. I said, "Well, you have to give me a chance to go get an oxygen tent or something…I can't breathe." She says "well, listen, write me something and send it to me, okay?" And I said, "Well, what do you want? Do you want a ballad? Or do you want something up? Do you want to be mid-range?" She said, "Do your thing." It was the most incredible, it was the most incredible thing ever.

> Amazing story by an amazing storyteller, right? I can envision Luther picking up the phone to hear the voice of the Queen, "Vandross."

BK: You have a lot of moments like that I can only imagine.

LUTHER: No.

BK: I mean, it's in my life. It's like there's moments I do an amazing interview or something at this point. Like, I'll come back next week. I did Luther. (did = interviewed) That's a cool moment for me. How did you keep reinventing your dream?

LUTHER: Yeah, you know. Well, the thing you do is you keep going on...they asked me what would I tell someone young who's about to enter show business or who wants to enter show business. And the first thing I say is to *make sure that you want to do it so that the rejections don't matter because it's a constant process of putting your face out there to be slapped. That's what it is. And you can't react to that. I never chose a plan B for myself, you know, my own personal plan was to do this or bust.* There was no plan B, there was no alternate plan of any kind. Because when rejection faces you, when you're faced with rejection, it pushes you closer to a plan B. And I didn't want there to be any chance that a Plan B would embrace me...And that's the philosophy I stuck to. I forgot the question.

BK: I don't know. But I like what you did with it...

LUTHER: [laughs] I was, that was a preface to something. But I lost...

BK: You started saying that you work with Aretha, Dionne and Diana. And I said, is it amazing how you have to keep reinventing.

LUTHER: Right, so what I meant to say was that you keep voting for yourself. You keep putting a ballot in the box, every morning, you get up and you put the ballot in the box, and you allow yourself to vote for yourself. And you do what you do. And some of it comes to you and some of it you have to go out and seize, you know? But you stay focused and you stay tunnel vision. And you stay one track-minded about it, you know? And I and a lot of other people who are successful would agree with that. That's the way to approach it.

> NO plan B is a common theme I have been recognizing and emphasizing. But Luther takes it a step further when he says "Vote for Yourself." I mean, everyone says "go out and vote," but it's much cooler when Luther says it. This is a movement I belong to...

BK: Last topic I want to talk about is touring. Your show is full of class, it's full style. Can you talk about your show, what is it about?

LUTHER: It's about the music first. The first thing that has to happen is that the music has got to be right. And it's got to be executed… the music demands the top dollar, you have to have the exact right staffing and the chemistry between the musicians and the singers. I decided way back that I wanted to give the person who took it upon himself to get out of the house and come to see me something to look at as well, you know? So we started doing that, the $20,000 gowns with the 2-foot trains and the staircases that lit each, you know a la Fred Astaire, when you walk up, each one would light, etc. And, you know, certainly an R&B, that type of extravagance was not the norm. And so

I spent a lot of money on gowns, staircases and coat racks that went up in the ceiling, and oh, floors that lit—you know, they're very expensive to present. But they endear people to you. See I like for somebody to know that you went the extra mile for them, you know, you go the extra effort, you do the extra stuff, you know, you don't come out with a flashlight and a microphone.

BK: There's a quote from Smokey (Robinson), "there are vocalists, and then there are Luther."

LUTHER: Oh yeah, I love Smokey.

BK: Everyone loves Smokey. Everyone loves Luther. The fact that the respect that you're getting from both the young and the old. We can just say "Luther" and we know who we're talking about.

LUTHER: It's one of the amazing, that's not a planned thing you know? I didn't set out about that, but it's great that Luther is a one name artist, you know? Aretha, Elvis, those are one name artists and it's really, really sensational. It's nothing that was planned. It's just, I think a reward for the dedication and for the…faithfulness to the gift that I was given. And I took the gift, and I was very honest with it. And the desire to please is just overwhelming.

To quote my personal mentor from afar Howard Stern, "Luther has done it all." But when I asked Luther what else was on his vision board—I kid as this was 1995 and that wasn't a thing. But I did ask about the future and he said he wanted to duet with Whitney. Of course I joked "oh that's really tough, like you can't make a phone call?" He said "it's a scheduling thing." But in true Luther fashion, he was so specific in what they wanted to do, it was going to be one up tempo and "one that would be the greatest ballad exchange you ever heard, and that's going to be fabulous." They never had that number one song together, Luther passed a decade later. But this is one pairing that I wouldn't be too upset if artificial intelligence helps us with.

He was an amazing talent, an amazing man and I was beyond fortunate to have a classic conversation with Luther Ronzoni Vandross. I interviewed Luther a second time in 2001 for his self-titled record on Clive Davis' new label at the time, J Records. I have the notes, but so bummed I cannot find the tape. I distinctly remember hugging it out at the album release party at the Four Seasons hotel on Doheny Drive in Beverly Hills. No wet bar or sunken living room, but Luther welcomed me with open arms. He had IT, whatever IT was.

REUNITED AND IT FEELS SO GOOD— ME AND LL A FEW YEARS AFTER OUR CONVERSATION, PROVING COOL NEVER GOES OUT OF STYLE.

DON'T CALL IT A COMEBACK, I'VE BEEN HERE FOR YEARS...

I'm not even gonna try to define what LL Cool J has meant to hip hop—and pop culture—from the '80s to now. Obviously, he's bigger than hip hop alone; he's a living, breathing cultural institution. Music, movies, television—he did it all. A spokesman, philanthropist, entrepreneur, he moves the needle and rocks the bells. His influence has stretched so far beyond the streets that even my grandmother knew who LL Cool J was.

The first time I interviewed James "Todd" Smith (LL Cool J) was in 1989, for his third album, Walking With A Panther. It was technically a commercial success, selling over a million copies, but it wasn't the blockbuster his label had hoped for and the hip hop community felt the same. It contained the track "Going Back to Cali" which is a personal favorite of mine, for its mantra and for the response, "I don't think so." Maybe it's because I was born in Brooklyn, living in Cali? "I don't think so."

I interviewed him a year later for the *Mama Said Knock You Out* album, and boom, LL Cool J was on top of the world, reigning champ. My first question to him was about the title track, asking if it was true that it was inspired by his grandmother. He confirmed, "We were watching TV, an award show. There was some singers or some rappers or something on the award show performing. She said 'those guys are pretty good. Y'all ain't doing nothing. You need to get on there and knock them out." I said "Alright, I made a song."

Wowza. My grandmother told me to watch what I eat. I didn't write a hit song—yet. But I am writing this book!

The third time I interviewed LL was in 1996 on the set of his hit TV sitcom, *In The House*. This was my favorite of the three as I got one of my mic drop BK celebrity stories. Here goes…

I arrived at the Hollywood soundstage where his show was taping, a production assistant greeted me and led me to a quiet area so I could set up my microphone and tape deck and be ready for the interview. Everything is normal so far. LL walks in and before we get down to business, he was hungry and we decided (he decided) we were gonna walk down the block to a Hollywood culinary institution—Roscoe's Chicken & Waffles.

Couple of notes on this. First off, when you walk the streets of Hollywood with LL, it's hilarious as there's lots of shout outs, honking horns, etc. I'm assuming the adulation was directed at him. Second, when you walk into Roscoe's with rap royalty, it's an experience. Funny aside, I'd been at that same Roscoe's just three days earlier, refueling after a Rippingtons concert at the Greek Theater. When I went solo, I couldn't decide on an order, and the server wasn't making it easier. But with Mr. Smith, the hospitality seas parted. I had a drink in my hand and a meal chosen for me within minutes. It's good to be the king, or king adjacent in my case. We ate, we drank (lemonade), and then headed back to the set to get down to business—the interview.

I was ready to rumble and had an agenda and topics to discuss: Martin Luther King (for a radio special I was writing), his TV show, and his new album which had a hit single "Hey Lover" with Boyz II Men that was charting. As mentioned before, it's always good to talk to an artist when their music is being well-received. I know, obvious. But why this chat was special to me is because we went from interview to conversation. I had questions planned out, but went into whatever direction he took me. Also, we both had been at this game for a minute, I knew what I needed and he knew how to deliver. His career was hot, but he had experienced some dips and his take on the roller-coaster ride was refreshing, life lesson type stuff. He was serving up knowledge, and I was devouring it just like I did the 1/2 chicken prepared southern style with two waffles. Thank you Roscoe's.

And thank you LL Cool J for lunch and a great chat. We got right into it, my recording level question was about MLK day, and LL had answers . My favorite quote was "the same people who hated him, gave him a holiday." Here's my conversation...

BK: Martin Luther King Day is coming up. And he means a lot to so many different people, so many different things for so many different people. When you were growing up a young kid in Queens, was that instilled in your house? Martin Luther King, what does he mean to you today?

LL: Martin Luther King to me symbolizes a man who was a great leader who stood behind his dreams and his visions, and wasn't afraid to dream—open his eyes and see what he wanted and go after it. And he was from a school of fighting fire with water not fighting fire with fire, which was an interesting approach. It may not necessarily always work. But most of the time it does, you know. And I think that he was very effective. And I think he broke a lot of ground in terms of how Afro Americans are treated in his day and time in America. And I think that all people—different religions, different races—would have faced persecution at different times in history. I think at this particular period of time, it's the Afro Americans turn to kind of feel that persecution. But at the same time, I think that what Martin Luther King showed is that, you know, "intellect" and "will" can defeat the greatest hate. And, I think that he's to be forever remembered for that.

BK: You brought up a great point fighting fire with water, you know, because I've talked to a couple people about this. And what they said is just like, they don't know to this day, if they were around back in the day, you know, like, they were able to do that. Sometimes it'd be like, wait a second, I can't do that.

LL: I mean, he had an interesting approach, his approach was nonviolent, that's deep. And you know, he died violently. However, I think that it is important that we utilize peaceful means. I mean, any general knows that sometimes it's necessary to go to war. I mean, sometimes it's unavoidable, that sometimes by trying to avoid war, you end up with a bigger problem later on. And then you're in a position to lose the war, you know? But at the same time, I think the key to a successful war—in terms of the kind of war a Martin Luther King waged—which was a war on hatred, and the war on racism, and separatism, and all of those different issues, I think the best way is to defeat your opponent without ever going to war. You know, it's by taking the mind of your opponent's army. You know, and I think that's what he did. He took a lot of people's minds and opened them up, and got them to think and realize what was going on. And subsequently, he's a celebrated man in this country. Saying, the same people that hated him, gave him a holiday.

BK: Second thing is the AMAs (American Music Awards). It's no secret that you're doing something for the AMAs, can you talk a little bit about what you got planned, what's going to happen?

LL: Well, I'm gonna perform. And I'm gonna do some songs and give people an opportunity to see what LL Cool J can do on stage, you know? When performing, just got to perform and have some fun, God willing. I mean, it's no secret we're gonna perform.

BK: You've been rocking the house for years seriously since your debut record, I mean you were a touring act. What about when you get in front of these awards audiences where it's a little bit different than the people, or is it different for you?

LL: They may not move a muscle, but you're not necessarily performing for, you know, for the 1,500 superstars that are sitting out front. Millions of people are watching that may enjoy your music or enjoy your performance. And for some, it isn't their taste, but that's why they call it the American Music Awards because it celebrates all of American music. And what I do is part of the music. I was born here in America. So there you go.

> Fun fact, I was covering those AMAs and saw LL Cool J rock the house with "Mama Said Knock You Out" and "Hey Lover." Guess who won Best Rap/Hip Hop Artist? Hint: Rhymes with Coolio...yes, Coolio.
>
> An excuse for me to tell a story.
>
> I had interviewed the "Gangsta's Paradise" rapper several times and he was a mainstay at many of the media events I produced. But my favorite Coolio story has nothing to do with either. Indulge me...I hired Coolio in 2006 to perform at the Cisco Systems sales convention in Las Vegas at the MGM Grand Arena. Cisco had a market cap north of $500 billion at the time, so budget wasn't an issue. But, this wasn't a normal performance, he had to rap new "Cisco inspired" lyrics and introduce CEO John Chambers to a rabid crowd of sixteen thousand employees from the company. And he knocked it out of the park. To witness him rap "when I say John, you say Chambers" and the crowd complied-that was a classic moment!!! I miss him, but I don't miss his TV show *"Coolio Rules."* No disrespect, but the reality show wasn't good at all. But LL Cool J's scripted TV show *"In The House"* was good, and I even watched it. See how I made that connect to bring us back?

BK: *In The House*, it's your show, actually one of the few shows that I've actually seen. I don't watch that much TV you know. I even saw the debut [he laughs]. And I even watched it again, which says something.

LL: That's cool.

BK: Right?

LL: Yeah it is, I don't watch television.

> I think we're bonding. First on chicken, now TV.

BK: Do you keep it light, because I also know that there is a serious side, you know, Todd, the businessman side, the suit. But can you keep it light, you are on a sitcom.

LL: There's no question about it. I mean, nothing wrong with being pleasant and having some fun. That doesn't like do anything to your serious side or put your integrity in jeopardy as long as you don't allow it to.

BK: What do you owe to the fact that the show is...

LL: Well first of all, I have to thank Quincy Jones and David Salzman for putting us in a position to do a show. I have to thank Debbie Allen for being willing to do the show with me. I have to thank people like Fresh Prince and Queen Latifah, and, you know, people who help pave the way so that a rapper can do a television show. I mean, you know, that's what I have to do. So, we're here now, we hope it lasts. If it doesn't, we'll move on to the next thing. But I'm thankful.

BK: Okay, now, I'll go generic on you real quick, the acting aspect of it. In fact, not to name drop, but I just interviewed Whitney Houston regarding *Waiting to Exhale* (huge name drop). And I said, same thing I said not to go generic on you. But let me ask you, what do you get from it, like, give me a little insight from the acting aspect of it.

LL: For me, I just get an opportunity to look at the world through different writers' eyes. I deal with different situations that I may not have necessarily dealt with in my life. So because of that, it makes me empathize with people who have been through things that I couldn't relate to before I was acting, you know, on a regular basis. And it helps you as a person, it helps you to grow because you deal with things that you may have never dealt with. You know, how does it feel for a mailman to come home and his wife is going through some trouble, you know, something that's happening? I mean, these are things that I never dealt with, I was never a mailman. But if I get an opportunity to play a mailman, then I can relate, at least relate and understand what it is that this man is going through. Or if I'm a construction worker, I can respect, you know, someone who does what they do for a living, and I can understand it better because I've played the part, I play the role, and I've seen how it affected me emotionally.

BK: Your character Marion is, I mean—not that I know you—but is kind of close to you in the sense that he has a background, a football player. Not that you're a football player, but we're just talking about… these football players, celebrities, music people, they kind of cross boundaries with each other. Give me a little insight on getting into the shoes of Marion.

LL: Marion is an interesting guy because he has all the right things, but sometimes he gets ahead of himself and seems to keep himself in a jam, which I learned I learned a lot from. I mean, like one episode Marion makes a comeback in football, he does so incredible. He's really successful. And then he gets cocky, he gets arrogant. And he leaves his family behind, his annex family, and he wants to hang out, have his crew, his posse now. He's raw, he's rugged, all of these things. And what happens is, he ends up injuring himself in a locker room. And now he's right back where he started. Whereas if he wouldn't have got arrogant and cocky and would have stayed with his annex family, he would have probably went on and been successful. See, I learned things from that. You know, because that tells me hey, when you're doing well, you know, just take it with a grain of salt. Because you have to understand that this too shall pass. You know? So that's the way I looked at.

> Dropping knowledge. Seriously, I was sitting there thinking, this kid has his act together. And we're the same age—yet I have no act, nor is it together. First, he's sharing powerful lessons from Martin Luther King about standing up to injustice. Then he offers a unique perspective on award shows from a performer's point of view. Now, he's using his "fun job" of acting to connect with others and gain insights that teach him valuable life lessons. It was a real teaching moment for me, one that still resonates today.

BK: Give me a little insight to your feelings on the record (*Mr. Smith*). You know what I mean? It's your new baby.

LL: I feel real good about it. I feel real, real good about it. I think that it was a joy to create. It was a lot of fun working with the people I worked with. Chris Lighty, Trackmasters, Rashad Smith, Chad Elliott, Easy Mo Bee, I mean, all of these people I work with on this album, all of the guest artists who came in and are a part of it. I mean, LeShaun, Foxy Brown, Fat Joe, Mobb Deep, Keith Murray. I mean, everybody who's on the album. I had a lot of fun with it— Boyz II Men.

BK: Yeah doesn't suck, you know? I mean, granted, if anyone could have been doing backing on that, you know, because the song ("Hey Lover") is a pretty good song. Actually, let's talk about the success. As we speak, it's still getting played.

LL: I mean, the reality is I had a song I wrote that I thought was good, you know? I thought that a great, great group singing it would make it a better song and a greater song. And they did that. That's what we did as far as the song is concerned, I love it.

BK: You surprised? Because I think it kind of went to number one on several charts. You know, there's about 30 different charts now covering urban music. But still, were you surprised by the fact that it kind of took off?

LL: Well, you know, it's interesting to me. I mean, I'm just thankful. I'm not really surprised, because I wouldn't underestimate myself like that. I knew what we did and what we were working with, and I felt good about it.

You know, sometimes I think that people have this image of, if a record doesn't make your nose bleed it's not going to do well. I don't know if it's the media or certain people they've come to feel that a rap record has to be hard or loud or wild for it to do well. Like you can't make a smooth record and it be credible which is totally untrue. That's why "I Need Love" was incredibly successful. That's why "Hey Lover" is doing the same thing. That's why "Around The Way Girl" did the same thing. Because people are always trying to pigeonhole and tell you what it is that they want you to do. They want your album to sound like they want it to sound. "If you don't yell on every record LL, your album's not credible." I make songs that I like and I enjoy, you know? I wanted to make a romantic song, I felt good about it. That's what we came out with first. It's that simple.

BK: That's awesome. *Mr. Smith* is your sixth record and when your previous records all kind of hit platinum, I mean you're hitting platinum platinum platinum. You got another one coming out, maybe a little nervous or pressure?

LL: Well, it's no pressure because the reality is that they don't always all do as well. The last one before this didn't do as good. *Mama Said Knock You Out* did real good. The one after that did okay, it didn't do really good. So the pressure is not really, see you can't get caught up in that. You just have to understand that whether it does well or doesn't, this too shall pass. And that's the way we have to move with it.

BK: I also want to talk about "Doing It," because I already heard it. It's got, you know, LeShaun. Give me a little insight to that track, how it came about?

LL: Well what happened was me and Chris Lighty had a meeting with the producer, Rashad, he had the track. I loved it, I thought it was great. And we had an idea to like, get the young lady who did a similar track long ago called "Doing it Well" and redo it. I would write a new song, but we use the same hook, a similar hook and do a new version. So I went in, I wrote it. LeShaun happened to call Chris during that time, and it worked out nicely. And we went in the studio and we recorded "Doing it."

BK: You have to wonder about sometimes like, almost like it's divine fate.

LL: All praises due to the Creator of all the world. There's no question about it. All praises due because I mean, the reality is that none of this would even be possible without the creation. The miracle of creation.

> Did "The Creator" hear the lyrics? I mean it's a pretty sexual song, leaving nothing to the imagination. I dug it for the shout-outs to Brooklyn, way before my birthplace was cool. And when the music video came out, I'm thinking what was up with him eating the apple? I "think" there's a metaphor or some symbolism there, but I digress...again.

BK: I've been interviewing people who are very successful the past six years, people like yourself, and I always wonder sometimes do you feel, I don't want to say guilty, but sometimes, like, maybe a little too blessed? Because, you know, you notice people in your situation give a lot of praise.

LL: Well, my praise goes to God. My praise goes to, you know, the divine Creator. And my thing is this you know, yeah, you CAN feel guilty. That's why when I see people laying in the street, I give them whatever I got. That's why I don't have a problem with giving things away. I'm not Scrooge, you know, it goes beyond what you say because I can say anything right now and be a hypocrite and be lying. My actions even speak more about my character.

BK: Good karma. Another thing I noticed, just by walking around with you, the response to you is actually wide range, which is pretty surprising. But all kind of like, "Hey LL" you know, Honk Honk "Nice to see you" which, you know, Mr. Hardcore rapper here. I'm just saying it's kind of surprising or is it?

LL: That hardcore rap thing, you know, it goes beyond that. You know what I'm doing, *I make rap music. I do television, not a hardcore rapper. I just make rap records. I do whatever I want to do as far as rap music is concerned. And I'm not afraid of the rap industry.* You know, I have no fear when I walk into the arena of rap. Whatever I'm doing, that doesn't mean that I'm always going to win, doesn't mean that I'm always going to succeed. But I have no fear. I can only fear God, you know. But at the same time, I'm not trying to be some type of tough guy either. That's not what my music is about. That's how I can put out "Hey Lover" and people could say, "Oh that's LL with Boyz II Men it's okay," you know? And then it blows up and it's exploding and it's platinum. And they like sitting in the mirror with Visine wondering, "Well, how did it happen? Oh my God LL did it," you know what I mean? Because it's not about all of that. I'm not caught up in all of that.

You see, I'm just trying to do what I do. I'm not going to allow the trends and people's personal emotions, and criticisms change the way I apply myself, you know. I'm going to pay attention to what's going on, but I'm going to apply myself a certain way. And I'm not going to be afraid to cry in a room full of people who cry in the dark, but won't cry in the light. See I cry in the light. You see what I'm saying?

BK: What about musically? Do you still get the same buzz creating that you did, like, ten years ago?

LL: No question about it, incredible, incredible. I don't listen to my albums over and over and over again like

I used to. I mean, once I make them it's pretty much, that's pretty much it. But I definitely get a buzz off of them. No question. I love it. I love making new records more than I like listening to them. Once they're done I don't even want to listen to 'em no more [laughs].

BK: LL, you've been a champ, like I knew you would. Thank you for taking time out.

LL: Cool.

To quote the king of ALL media Howard Stern, "he said it all." That was the final time conversating with Todd, but I have been fortunate enough to see him a few more times at events, including the Radio Music Awards where we snapped a quick photo (he looks good, I not so much).

He's put out more albums since then. They may not all hit platinum heights, but LL's legacy doesn't hinge on chart positions. LL makes music because he can—and because he's still doin it and doin it well, the "Ladies Love Cool James." I think everyone loves "LL" and so do I.

Photo: Bobby Quillard

"I DID INTERVIEW USHER, BUT DIDN'T THINK HE WAS "BIG ENOUGH" FOR MY 1ST BOOK. OUR HANDS EXPLAIN WHICH BOOK HE SHOULD BE A PART OF."

BUSHI

WHEN YOU CAN'T FIND MISSY, LET BUSTA DO THE TALKING—JUST LIKE HE DID ON THE FIRST AND LAST TRACKS TO HER DEBUT ALBUM, SUPA DUPA FLY.

HOW WOULD I DESCRIBE MISSY ELLIOTT?

The terms trailblazer, trendsetter and unique come to mind. But notice these descriptions blend into just one, "an original." The reality is that Missy described herself for me with the release of her debut album, *Supa Dupa Fly*…she wasn't just "fly," she was "supa dupa fly."

There was nobody like Missy in the late '90s. A relative unknown outside the music industry, she was already making a name for herself as a writer and collaborator with another Virginia born original, Timbaland. I feel their big break came when they helped craft and produce a good portion of Aaliyah's sophomore album, *One in a Million*. Success breeds success.

Missy wasn't the first to go from songwriter-producer to "artist," but she did redefine what it meant to be an "artist" in hip hop and R&B. I was impressed with her lyrical prowess, crafting verses that were as playful as they were profound. Her collaboration with Timbaland introduced futuristic sound—pulsating beats, off-kilter rhythms, and innovative production—that instantly set her apart.

At the same time, she revolutionized visual artistry in music, making her an MTV icon. Together, these elements created a wholly unique and impactful presence that immediately positioned her as a game-changer and one of the most exciting artists of her time.

But I didn't know any of that when I met her at Elektra Records at 345 Maple Drive in Beverly Hills. All I knew is she had a presence. She had style, her own style. She had personality for days. And more importantly for me at the time, she had a hit record. So instead of interviewing her before the initial rise, I was talking to her in real time as it was happening. This was exciting for me after almost a decade of interviewing "celebrities."

I knew she was a star, not breaking any ground there. What I didn't know then was that, like many innovators blessed with an outsized dose of talent, she'd end up in the Rock & Roll Hall of Fame. Really? I'm one of those music critics who think the "rock hall" should be dedicated to "rock" artists and have often bristled at the politics of their inductions (Kate Bush?), and their non-inductions of artists that have made an impact in music. But since they opened the doors to rap — full disclosure, I produced the Run DMC after party in Cleveland in 2009 — I get that Missy "Misdemeanor" Elliott deserves her spot among the cream of the crop.

The only thing I didn't get was her adopted nickname "Misdemeanor," which was supposed to encapsulate her bold, mischievous and innovative persona. If that's the case, why not "felony" which would denote a more serious talent, right? I know, it doesn't roll off the tongue and I think the music gods heard my prayers as we are now able to drop nicknames and even last names as today, there's only one Missy. And I had only one interview with her, and it was a classic conversation.

BK: My first question is the fact that you are probably one of the best known secrets in the R&B community for a few years. But the reality is that the secret's out. Give me a little insight from your perspective, because you're still on this ride as we speak. What's it been like?

MISSY: What has it been like? In the beginning trying to get where I'm at now, it was kind of rocky and depressing. But where I'm at now is cool. I mean, I'm not too large. And I'm not that low, where people don't know who I am, I'm in the middle so that's cool. Give me room to grow.

BK: All right, what kept you going?

MISSY: Believing in God. I'm a true believer that if it's meant, then it's meant and I'm gonna keep going. If I feel like that strong about my talent, then I wasn't gonna let anybody stand in the way and make me think otherwise.

In the beginning, a lot of people didn't have that much faith in me and I had to, like, have faith in myself to get where I'm at and have faith in God that he would allow me to be right here. And that's what happens, it's faith.

BK: Can you describe what you're going through? I mean, this whirlwind around you is pretty amazing. I mean is there any way to, in a sense sum up like, what a rise to fame is like?

MISSY: Nah, unless you got days [chuckle]. Um, a rise to fame… I mean, everybody has had their different rise to fame. I mean, like I said, *I went from depressed to "Okay, it's gonna work" to "I'm here." You know, that's basically my rise to fame.* Very, very depressing at first.

Like I said, I had a lot of people who didn't have that much faith in me. And then with faith in myself, I got to a point where, "Okay, maybe this can work." And to people starting to believe in my talent, and then from the energy of people believing that I could make it to where I'm at right now, after I realized that I had some fans out there from the little stuff that I did do. It made me feel like well, if I keep going, then I could be right here. And so that's where I'm at.

BK: Ain't that bad. Listen I mean right here with me ain't that bad. Alright, so I'm not going to ask you to describe what's been going on or what has been the biggest surprise because you know, you and I, even when we were little kids, you dream of stuff like this. When it kind of happens, there's no book that says, "Well, this is what you do, and this is how it is." What was the biggest surprise of consecutively hitting?

MISSY: The biggest surprises, getting nominated for a lot of these awards like MTV, Grammys, Soul Train, NAACP. All those was like dreams when I was little, you know, just from me being little watching TV and seeing people like Michael Jackson performing at MTV or the Grammys, and now being a part of that audience. That's like, the big thing for me.

BK: That was one of my questions, did you watch awards shows growing up?

MISSY: I think everybody did. Anybody who's involved in like being nominated for any of these awards, I believe that it was a dream, to every last one of the artists that is involved in it now.

BK: Let me tell you, specifically, let's talk Grammys. Grammys is the granddaddy...few years ago, they wouldn't be recognizing people like yourself. And, you know, not only do they recognize you, but they really recognize you this year. Talk to me about The Grammy Awards, what's going to happen, what you want to see.

MISSY: Huh, what I want to see at the Grammys? I want to see me walk away with an award. That's what I want to see at the Grammys. But performance wise, I like to see different performances, I don't know who's performing at this Grammy. I remember growing up watching, like different awards, used to watch to see the performances and used to watch to see what people had on [chuckles]. So that's like another part of it and to see who'll walk away with an award. You know, in my case, if I don't win, I'm not mad because this is like my first record of my own. And to be involved in all of these awards is like a big deal to me. Because people who are doing their junior album, or have done a sophomore album, haven't even gotten nominated for a lot of these awards. So, you know, it's cool just being there.

BK: Let's talk a different subject. Let's talk *Soul Train*. Now growing up, you must have I mean, everyone, or were you not allowed to watch *Soul Train*?

MISSY: I was allowed to watch *Soul Train*. But if *Soul Train* went over the time that it was for me to go to bed, then I couldn't see the ending of *Soul Train*. I was allowed to watch *Soul Train* though.

BK: I mean, let's be honest, talking about music, fashion—I mean, did you religiously watch it? Did you think someday or…

MISSY: Um, me watching it? I always, like I tell everybody, my imagination is like so major because when I was little, I used to watch other artists but envision myself being a person that's going up there getting awards. So, I always had like one of those imaginations to put myself in a place of that person. So, it was almost like I foreseen this right here. You know, it was other people getting it, but I always said, I'm gonna be up there someday, you know, whether I'm getting it or whether I'm there, so.

BK: When you foresaw our interview, you hanging with Barry, was I this good looking?

> Looks creepy in print, probably sounded creepy in person. But she laughed, she gets me!

MISSY: [Laughs] Yeah, I just thought you would have had on another outfit like some jeans or something.

BK: Well, actually, I would have… I had a meeting today, this morning, trust me, you know, I'm usually more like that.

MISSY: Okay. Okay.

> I wish I had a picture of me and Missy from that day as I am dying to remember what I had on, must have been fancier than normal.

BK: All right. Well let's talk about a topic that you've been asked a lot since you first came on the scene. I mean, you're a songwriter, you're an arranger, you're a producer, you're a singer, you're a rapper, you kind of do it all. What don't you do?

MISSY: I don't play the violin [laughs].

BK: Doesn't mean that you won't take lessons, I hope.

MISSY: Nah, I'll just sit back and let somebody else do that. I'll let you do that.

BK: Alright…you made a major mark as a writer, you know, what do you get from writing that you maybe don't get from performing, that you don't get from making a record you know.

MISSY: Um, writing, what I get from that is being able to express how I feel. And performing you can express how you feel. But in writing it's your words, and people they can relate to like what you're saying. And a lot of people may have been through situations like that. So, I like to write because I like to touch, you know, topics and subjects that people go through in everyday life. I write like a lot of street slang that people use out on the street, not so much bad grammar, but just the way like if you with one of your home girls, or home boys, you kicking it. The type, the way you would talk to one of your friends. And I put that in the song for 'em so people can kind of relate to it.

BK: Hey Missy, let's just put it this way, I needed a dictionary on some of these things [laughs]. And I'm down, if you know what I'm saying, there's definitely some things that I don't know [Missy still laughing]. Alright…more on songwriting. When you're writing back in the day, are you writing for yourself or are you writing to fit, whether it's an Aaliyah or whether it's, you know…

MISSY: Nah, when I write I just write songs, and it's just songs, and if the artists like it, then I'll give it to 'em. It's not like, you know, if somebody comes to me and say, "Well, I need you to write for Aaliyah," that I will write a "Back and Forth." Or if they say, "We want you to write a song for Brandy," I'm not gonna go and try to write a song, like, "I Want To Be Down," I'm gonna write just a song that I would write for myself. And I think that's what makes the artists look good, because it's like, okay, you kind of put them on a whole 'nother level. Because, like, people listened to "Can We" and say, that don't sound like SWV…so, it made people like, really pay attention to it. And I'd rather do songs like that than do they typical songs that they always been known to do.

BK: When did people start paying attention to you? They talk about this music industry, in general, is a tough industry.

MISSY: Right.

BK: Then they talked about, you know, a woman even getting heard if you will. And then let's just talk about a Black woman.

MISSY: Right.

> What's sort of interesting about this line of questioning in the '90s is that it highlights that there weren't many artists like Missy, writing and producing for others as well as herself. Hence, the descriptions I initially gave—trailblazer, trendsetter, and unique—were appropriate.

BK: So, when did people start saying, was it like, when you had a hit song? Or when did they say "All right, you know…"

MISSY: Well a lot of people didn't know I was the person behind these songs, so it really wasn't talked about until "The Rain" came out. And then people like, you know, when they were doing interviews, they might have got the bio seeing okay, she wrote "One in a Million," "4 Page Letter,"

"What About Us?," Ginuwine, whoever. And then it started circulating, this business is not as big as people think it is. So, it starts circulating around that, "Okay, she did this song, she did that song," or whatever. So, a lot of people didn't know, they knew they liked the songs, but they didn't never pay attention to who wrote it, so.

BK: All right [Missy chuckles]. So another common question that people ask you, because this is our first interview with you, the whole idea of the singing, versus the rapping, you know. Usually when I'm talking to someone, like, you know, I interviewed Aaliyah for that record, she ain't kicking raps. She's known as a singer. What about the fact that you're multifaceted?

MISSY: Uhhh.

BK: In other words, you know, how does that happen? You know, that usually doesn't happen with most artists.

MISSY: How does that happen?

BK: Both, why and how did you make it happen?

MISSY: Um, how it happened is God given talent. Why did I make it happen is because no one had ever did it. I mean, you have people to do it, but they didn't like keep it going on. Like Lauryn (Hill) is a beautiful singer and she raps along with Latifah you know. And I felt like they done it and maybe they just, you know, it might not have been going in the direction that they want it to go so they kind of like wanting to stick with one thing. And I felt like on the other hand, since no one else has really taken it there, let me just use all of them to that advantage. When people think I'm a rapper then I'm gonna come with a singing song that's gonna make people be like, "Whoa man, she do it all." So you know, just trying to do whatever no one else is doing.

BK: Well, let me ask you this, because an obvious question to me is that you didn't grow up in LA, you didn't grow up in New York, and, you didn't even grow up in Atlanta. There I said it, you know, the music mecca these days.

MISSY: Right.

BK: Let me just throw that out there. I mean, what, what does that give you? Like, what was that like? And what does that mean? You know, what does that give you musically, you know, growing up in Virginia?

MISSY: Um, I think that just shows that it's a lot of talent, other places, besides the main markets like New York and LA, and Atlanta, cause those been like, the main places where a lot of artists have been founded from, you know? But, um, that just shows that we're overlooking a lot of talent that's in these little states. And as far as me, I'm trying to put Virginia on the map as like one of those other states that has talent.

So Timbaland, he push our little state in there too. And it was different because we didn't get songs as quick as other states. So, you know, I think that's another reason why our sound is different, because we never, like we had to make up our own sound because we never got songs that quick to know what was hot and what wasn't.

BK: Right. I mean, could it be safe to say that there's almost a Virginia sound?

MISSY: Yeah, it's a Virginia sound.

BK: Is it laid back? How do you…

MISSY: Very laid back. Virginia is very laid back, relaxed. If you listen to most of the beats that we do, they're very laid back. Like instead of them being like club pop dance beats, they like songs you ride down the street, you just bop your head to whatever. So it's a very laid back feel.

BK: Missy what was your childhood like?

MISSY: Um, I had a fun childhood. I mean, I'm, like I said, I'm one with a very wild imagination. I was the only child. So I had to make up a lot of games by myself, because my mother was a…well, my father was in the Navy at the time, my mother was at work. So, a lot of times, I had to make up things for myself and games. Listening to songs and envision myself doing a video and all that. So it was cool and all. I think if it wasn't for me having to make up a lot of the things that I've done, I don't think I'll be here. I think I'll be just doing a regular job. But I had, my imagination was so "wow" that it was almost like I had to see up until now that this is where I would be. Because I always wanted to be an entertainer. Like, I used to let videos keep me or rock me to sleep. You know?

> Now THAT is funny. I mean, there's no way I could be rocked to sleep watching a Missy Elliott music video. I think using her videos to wake up makes more sense. Could you imagine falling asleep to "Lose Control," "Work It" or "Get Ur Freak On"?

BK: Let's be honest, because I know music hit me pretty early. I mean, I would imagine music hit you pretty early too. And if so, was it your mom's influence on you or… how did you get the music in you?

MISSY: Well, my mother used to sing a lot. But like I said, a lot of times back when I was growing up, like during high school, we used to listen to a lot of different songs like Houdini, Run DMC, LL [Cool J], you know, and so that had a lot to do with it. And a lot of kids that was around me were like really into music. So a lot of my friends by them being into music got me into music. But my mother was always a singer. So like going to church, and watching my mother sing every Sunday got me into it.

BK: Well, I thought, would it be safe to say, you had a church background?

MISSY: I was definitely, my mother's very, very religious. I was in church every Sunday. No church, no play.

BK: I've interviewed so many people and they talked about like, you know, if you grew up singing in the church, there's a difference. There's a feeling. I mean, can you relate?

MISSY: Yeah, I believe that. I know like, because in church when you singing a gospel song in church, you see like a lot of people they really put a feeling into it. They started crying. And I believe that like growing up in a church, you can kind of tell people who had a church background, you know, just by the way they sing too. I mean, it's so many different ways that you could tell a person had a church background, faithfully.

BK: Yeah, I was gonna say one of the best things about churches that generally when you get up there, they're supportive. So, they kind of make you…

MISSY: Right.

BK: You know, it kind of keeps you going. And you're like, "Yeah, I can do this." You know, you brought up a pretty interesting point in one of your first answers, and you're saying something like, you know, like I envisioned it or something. Like, you know a lot of people maybe sometimes don't think they're good enough.

MISSY: Mhm.

BK: Or you know, maybe not, you know. I'm writing the songs, but no one's listening.

MISSY: Right.

BK: But are you one of the people who were, because you see, I've seen you on talk shows before, you're a little quiet. But I have a feeling when you're with your friends, you're not that quiet.

MISSY: Oh no.

BK: You know what I'm talking about? Then, what are you? Did you believe, did you think you had something to offer? Or was it more like…

MISSY: Yeah, I believe I had something to offer…I used to always be like, very musical in school. I wasn't in school choir, but like everybody, I used to do a lot of talent shows. So, I believe that it was something there, it just had to fall into the right hands.

BK: Oh, yeah, they talked about how you used to perform on like…

MISSY: Trash can.

BK: Trash can, what's the deal with that?

MISSY: Like I said, a kid with a wild imagination. I used to get on garbage cans and I would like to sit all my doll babies up against the wall and just sing to them and put in my mind that they were clapping, or they were screaming my name, and stuff like that.

> Another artist manifesting way before that was a thing. Singing in front of the mirror is nothing new, setting up dolls on trash cans as the audience is next level.

BK: What do you consider the big break? I'm not talking about the recent thing, right? But like, what was the big break back in the day? Was it when you were with the other group Sista?

MISSY: Yeah, that was a big break.

> Missy was a member of the R&B girl group Sista in the early '90s, who were part of the larger musical collective Swing Mob—led by DeVanté Swing of Jodeci. They put an album out on Elektra Records which didn't get much "love" in the industry, but that's where she initially met and collaborated with Swing Mob cohort Timbaland to work on songwriting and production for other acts, yielding commercially successful releases for 702, SWV, Total and of course, Aaliyah.
>
> Fun fact, Mr. "Ride The Pony" himself Ginuwine was also a part of Swing Mob.

BK: Well, you know, I was making fun about you. I know your voice, but you know, everyone talks about that laugh. You know, you've had that laugh a couple of times in this because I am funny, no doubt [Missy chuckles]. But it's something. Is it shocking to you or weird to you that people comment on the fact that you have like, almost in a sense a trademark laugh now?

MISSY: It's funny. It's funny, but I guess it is like that. It's like a habit. I probably have done it over 25 times and didn't even notice it, but…

> Just say it Missy, I'm funny…just ask me.

BK: That's cool. Where does "Misdemeanor" come from?

MISSY: Magoo gave me that name like 10 years ago, and it didn't mean anything. He just thought it was cute. So, I kept it ever since.

BK: Has it come to mean anything?

MISSY: Nah, nah it's just there.

BK: All right. So, you bought up Timbaland a couple times. And I have to ask you, you know, first of all when did you meet him? And how did that musical relationship develop?

MISSY: I met Timbaland maybe like 10 years ago and that developed just by us being around each other, like a lot. He was under Devanté, too. And we moved to Rochester, we moved to Jersey. So, we were always in the studio with DeVanté. And we used to do like, make songs together just to have and just to ride down the street and listen to. So, we just continue to do that. And here we are.

BK: The album came out and then went platinum. And it's still selling. The fact that your album, out of the box kind of did probably better than a lot of people expected, believe it or not. I mean, I know anyone who gets a platinum record is pretty amazing. What are your feelings on the fact that it did hit?

MISSY: I'm just blessed. I mean, I didn't do it to say, "I will be platinum, double platinum." I did it for my fans and just doing it you know, just to put it out there because I was getting so many, like, people asking me, "When you gonna do an album? You know, you always guest appearing, can you do a whole album? Blah blah, whatever." So, I just did off the strength of that. And, you know, by being platinum plus, that's cool. I ain't mad at all.

BK: I know, I wouldn't be mad either. So what are the plans for the next record?

MISSY: Um, same thing, just doing it. I don't like to, like, plan too much on it. Because then you start thinking too hard, and it doesn't become real. So if you just do it off of the strength, then I think you turn out with a good album that way. Instead of just like thinking real hard, like, "It's got to be better than this last one." Just do it.

> Preach!

BK: Have you changed your way from writing songs back in the day? I mean, have you been learning? You're still young.

MISSY: Yeah. You change everything, whether you try to or not, you change the clothes, you change the hair. So it's automatic that, like, I listen to songs that I used to do and see the big difference in how I wrote back then, and how I write right now. Because back then I thought the way I wrote was hot. You know and now I listen to it and I'll be like, "What were you talking about?" you know. And I might change my whole writing style for this next album and listen to this album and think, like, you know, it wasn't as hard as I thought. I mean, it's got to fit for its time.

> She sounds like a veteran, a wise one so to speak. What insight, it's an amazing thought from someone who is at the beginning of her career. Music has got to fit for its time.

BK: With a lot of people, you know, they're talking about "When are you gonna do an album?" You know what, when we gonna see you performing again? Give me a little insight, because you know, you grew up performing. What do you get from performing in front of people, what's that feeling that it gives you?

MISSY: Um, I just be amped. I get real geeked from performing in front of a large crowd, because it's like, I get to see how much they really enjoy watching me perform, and how much they really love my music. Because if I'm out there, and I'm performing, it makes me work harder when I look out in the audience and see people singing the words to my song or screaming. So, it's like "A-ha." A natural "A-ha."

> Definitely better performing in front of a crowd than performing on garbage cans in front of her dolls.

BK: Who keeps you grounded? Is it family?

MISSY: My mother.

MISSY ELLIOT 203

BK: I mean, because there's no book that's written on fame...soon you believe you can do anything yet there's always that one person that says, "Missy."

MISSY: Yeah, my mother.

BK: How close I mean, give me a little insight to what she feels about what's been happening with your career.

MISSY: My mother, she's very excited. But she's still my mother. And when I go home, I'm still washing dishes. I'm still cleaning my room. So to the world I might be Missy "Misdemeanor" Elliott and to her "Missy get in here and clean your room or wash these dishes." So at the same time you know, I might go out in the street and feel you know, "Wow, I'm really a star." When I go home it's like I'm a star, but you're not too much of a star to get in here and clean up. And that's what I like about my mother is that she keeps my feet on the ground. I'm straight and I don't get out of hand and start disrespecting people.

BK: Well, let's talk about the star aspect. Your celebrity is actually kind of good celebrity. Because it's kind of like, I was talking to Mary J, not to you know drop names. But like, people that come to Mary J are true, like, you know, like, they feel it. And I would imagine the same people, I mean, it's usually out of sincere love. When did you first realize that you were touching people like that? What does that mean for you?

MISSY: I mean, this is a beautiful thing to know that what I'm doing is not in vain. And that people are listening. And people do recognize and love what I do. And like when people come up to me and be like, you know, "My little girl she loves your videos, and she's singing your songs." It's cool to see that I can feel some kind of assistance to people like you know, maybe my song made somebody happy. Or you know, make somebody leave somebody that was playing on them, cheated on or whatever.

BK: I don't think you ever get over hearing your music on the radio, do you?

MISSY: Nah you shouldn't never get over hearing your music on the radio. That's your money.

BK: What do you spend your money on? Because I know some of the clothes you get. I mean, let's be honest, the Nike jackets, even if you bought in the store, they're not that expensive. What's the one thing that gets you?

MISSY: Cars. Cars.

BK: How are you as a driver?

MISSY: Um, my mother said I drive too fast. But I think I drive cool.

BK: Listen, I remember when I bought my first car, you probably know when you bought your first seven. [Missy laughs]

BK: All right, what about the future future? What are the things that I don't know about? What are you striving to do? What are you striving to be? Because it's still early.

MISSY: Um, well, I'm just taking it a day at a time. You know, when I get there, I get there. A lot of people like to plan like, really, really far ahead…. but I just rather take it year by year I guess.

BK: All right, my last question. What's it like meeting some of your heroes? You know what I mean? Like you mentioned you grew up listening to LL [Cool J] and then boom, you know, you're gonna be at an award show. And there's LL.

MISSY: I mean that's like a dream and a dream come true. And it just goes to show that I've accomplished a lot of, like, dreams that I always had when I was little. To be able to, to sit two seats across from Janet Jackson, or to be at the concession stand with Michael Jackson or to even talk to people like Salt-N-Pepa because I'm a big Salt-N-Pepa fan. And, when I met them, they were just as excited to see me as I was to see them…so, you know, it's cool.

BK: That's cool. It sounds like even though you want to say you take it day by day, the reality is, it sounds like you're in this for longevity.

MISSY: Oh, yeah, most definitely. Most definitely. I'm in it for longevity.

BK: All right. Listen, Missy. It's a friggin pleasure. I was writing about you for a few years, a few years ago. And now it's just, it's really sweet to see the record take off. I'm very happy for you.

MISSY: Thank you. Thank you.

No, thank you! At the beginning of my conversation about Missy I asked "how would I describe her?" I came up with "an original." After revisiting this interview, I think it still fits. I heard a young woman who knew what she wanted to do, what she wanted to be as a child and then set forth on the journey. But at the same time, she was practical in her thinking and planning or dare I say lack of planning. To paraphrase her advice, "don't think, just do it." I personally relate to this a little too much as thinking, planning, and obsessing over my game plan, or lining all the ducks up in a row has actually stymied my creative process. I used it as an excuse to be consumed over minute details when in reality, it's been a safety mechanism to protect me from failure or what I would perceive as failure. I've been thinking about writing a book for years. I have the content, the stories and anecdotes, but always found an excuse to postpone. It took a classic conversation to realize that I should "just do it." I suggest we all take Missy's advice.

HEADSET ON, GAME FACE READY—
JUST ME MULTITASKING WITH HOVA,
PROVING EVEN THE BIGGEST NAMES
IN RAP CAN'T STOP THE HUSTLE.

JAY-Z... IT DOESN'T GET MUCH BIGGER IN HIP HOP. When you have the opportunity to talk about an extended chat you had with one of the major heavyweights in music, it's hard not to include this chapter in the book (and in my life).

And this all happened before he was a leader in business, philanthropy—and oh yeah a billionaire who married Queen Bey.

I met Jay-Z in early 2000 at the west coast offices of Island Def Jam records, a week before the release of his fourth album *Vol. 3… Life and Times* of S. Carter. I came in as a fan having already played his first three albums in heavy rotation, with his "Can I Get A What What" being an office anthem. I wasn't reviewing, just promoting which is a good thing because I didn't "love" this album as much. But what did I know? The album debuted that week at number one on the Billboard album charts.

We bonded over Brooklyn, our shared birthplace, and I knew right then that this kid had a plan—a blueprint, you could say—even before he made an album by that name.

He made some bad decisions and had some challenges along the way, we even alluded to his arrest a month earlier, but I decided to keep it light as I wasn't Geraldo Rivera, breaking news. I was just there to chat with an artist before he was a music mogul, before there was a Roc Nation, when he was just Jay and I was just B.

BK: By the way, congratulations.

JAY-Z: Thanks, man.

BK: You know what I mean.

JAY-Z: Yeah.

> Interview 101, butter them up before the hard-hitting questions.

BK: I guess that's how I'm going to start the interview. There's nothing better when I'm talking to an artist, we don't know what's going to happen. And there's a lot of hype, there's a lot of speculation. Well, you still don't know.

JAY-Z: Right.

BK: You kind of came out, you did all right! [Jay laughs] Talk to me a little bit about the feelings, the emotions, the fact that the record kind of came out and did what some thought it may do.

JAY-Z: I mean, I think we picked the wrong data, we could have did a lot more. But I'm happy with the number one record, you know, the millennium. It's just a good thing, man. Like every record, every record I've done I've shown progress you know what I'm saying? I feel that each way creatively and economically, you know, it just has been steps for me. I set my foundation, like, first album was a gold album, you know, which I felt my best album was the least selling album, you know, I mean, go figure. Second album a platinum album, next album, five million. This album the jury's still out, who knows, you know what I'm saying? It's just been a growth for me. And I just, I'm happy with my career, the way it's been going.

BK: The reality is, I mean, I've been doing this for a while. I didn't dress up today. [Jay chuckles] But I've been doing interviews for a long time. And the reality is, a lot of times, there's young cats that come out and they just blow up the first record and it's like multi-platinum, one track…I mean, there's very few artists, except for the rock genre, where it builds into a career. Can you talk about that aspect of it? Or maybe you're in it and you can't realize it?

JAY-Z: Yeah, it's just like you said, a growth period, you know what I'm saying? I had to deal with hardships and everything, all that, you know. I had to deal with everything. So it's no time for a swelled head or no time to get relaxed, because I know it could go either way at any time.

BK: Well, let's be honest. Before this record came out, there was a lot written about the quote, unquote, pressure, and even there were some quotes from you talking about, you know, I don't know how I'm gonna live up to the last record.

JAY-Z: Right.

BK: As far as digits. I mean, it's an obvious question. Let's be honest, when you have a record that

does as well as the last record, kind of tough…
or what did you do, did you just focus or?

JAY-Z: Yeah, I just went back and I just say, yo I know what I gotta do, man. I can't just make music, you know, happy music or whatever music, just safe music. I gotta go back to my form. I got to experiment with different sounding tracks. I gotta stay to my formula. I got to make sure that I'm happy with the album at the end of the day. Because you know, it's no telling if I can meet five million again. So what will make me happy if I don't make five million? If I made an album that I can play, and I can listen to be like…I know what's hot, you know what I'm saying?

BK: Well, that was it. Again, one would assume you have such a successful record, like the last record, that the tracks that you would be getting…it's kind of like a Tom Hanks thing you know. Tom Hanks gets the best roles because he's Tom Hanks. You may get some of the best tracks, you know. What was that like with the almost, in a sense, feeding frenzy on Jay-Z.

JAY-Z: Right. I took myself out of that, you know what I'm saying like I always do. I went with Timbaland you know, he was my choice. And I told him "Yo, bring me some tracks like you've never done before. I want to hear some different sounding music from you," you know what I'm saying? We challenged each other in the studio, you know, and that was like the bulk of the album. Like he did like four tracks on there. And then I just went back to Premier (DJ Premier) as always, you know, he's gonna give you that "pom pom," he's gonna give you that gutta.

BK: One of the things that I noticed again is that there was something different. But there's definitely a distinct sound right now for a Jay-Z record. There really is. Maybe it's your voice. Maybe it's the style that you're rappin', I have no idea. But I mean, let's be honest, I know when I was driving in the car and heard the single, kind of knew it was Jay-Z. Is that something that just is natural? Or is it, I mean, I don't think you work on it.

JAY-Z: It just is, it's me. I don't write lyrics down. So it's really just, I vibe with a track. And I guess it's that Jay-Z vibe that's coming off the track you know what I'm saying.

BK: I mean, there's some high profile rappers a couple years ago that are not as high profile. I'm not gonna mention names because I like some of them. [Jay chuckles and agrees] Is there something that you know, some insight into the fact that you know what the people want, or what?

JAY-Z: *I try to plug into you. If you could just flow right on a track, and you can pick a topic that everyone can relate to, then I mean half the job is done.* Now, what you got to do is just bring people real close to the story. You can't just talk about it, you got to bring them real close. You got to talk about the details in the story. You got to really take it there. You know, I mean, you can't just be lazy, like and just tell the story, you got to *tell* a story.

> Preach! This is the rap theory of "the devil is in the details." The most important or crucial aspects of the lyrics can be found in the small, seemingly insignificant details. Jay is painting a picture with his lyrics.

BK: The title of the record is *The Life and Times of S. Carter*. Tell me the difference between Shawn and Jay.

JAY-Z: It's just, I guess what Jay-Z is as far as recording, the recording is very, very arrogant, because there's a confidence that I have with my music, you know, because the way I came into it. Like when I first came here with *Reasonable Doubt*, no one would sign me, you know? I could have easily said like, "I must be not hot." When in turn, I took myself one against a whole machine, it was like, they don't know what they're talking about. That's a tough thing to do for a kid just coming into a business you know what I'm saying? So it just says there's a little more confidence in Jay-Z.

> I have heard this story hundreds of times, countless artists who were told their music was subpar. Music is an art form that is subjective, it's either good or bad. But the takeaway we get here is the mantra I practice and preach: believe in yourself.
>
> Motown founder Berry Gordy, who I have had the honor to interview and meet a few times, was the personification of "bet on yourself." And for Jay and many a focused creative, there's no plan B. Jay here, took his rejection as rocket fuel to manifest his creative dreams. Okay, full disclosure here, I'm not a new age guru, and it pained me to write "manifest his creative dreams." I was paraphrasing fancy, "the music labels don't know shit."

BK: Has Jay-Z changed? Or has Jay-Z's friends changed?

JAY-Z: Jay-Z is the same person, you know, I wouldn't say

my friends changed. I just got the same friends. I say people outside of my circle have changed. You know, it's like they treat you different, and then they expect you to act the same. You vibe with people the way they are with you, you know what I'm saying? So, Jay-Z hasn't changed, not with his friends that's inner circle. People outside of the circle, definitely will say I've changed because they've changed.

BK: Let's be honest, you've also gotten a lot better looking.

> I've used this joke a number of times in my interviews, as in mo' money, mo' models. But I throw it out there because I have witnessed this phenomenon in person many times (yes, in the Boyz II Men classic conversation).
>
> My favorite instance is when I was interviewing an artist named Timmy T, who had a number one record in 1991 with the song "One More Try." Now, he's a good looking man today but back in 1991, he was not. I'm not a looker either, but he had several beautiful girls trying to get his attention, waiting for him, while I was doing the interview. All I could think to myself at the time was "I should have kept playing the drums." But Jay takes the high road with his answer, and he's 100% right.

JAY-Z: I mean, attractiveness is not always physical, not a physical thing you know what I'm saying. They can be attracted to the confidence, attracted to the way I carry myself, you know, they might think I'm charismatic, you know, it's a lot of different things to being attractive you know what I'm saying so that can have something to do with it. I've thought about this before, once or twice. [Jay chuckles]

BK: What about the fact, let's be honest, you are the franchise player. You are a partner in Roc-A-Fella. How do you keep yourself as an artist as opposed to quote unquote, businessman?

JAY-Z: When I'm an artist, I'm an artist first and foremost, you know. Which is the best thing and it happens because you make the music before you can market it and promote it. So I get a chance to really be an artist. Then after I'm finished, I'm like, okay, what's the single? What's this? Well, how are we gonna do that? How are we gonna market, you know what I'm saying? So it works perfectly for me.

BK: In a sense, you went from what we call you know, an underground artist to people in the suburbs that are very familiar with Jay. What's that experience like?

JAY-Z: Right. That one, it's amazing to me like, and the age groups right now is amazing. Like guys, business executives with suits are like, "Jay-Z, love the record, man." I'm like, wow.

BK: Now also, you're a young kid from Marcy projects. I'm from Bayside originally. Let's be honest, who knew you were gonna be traveling the world? I mean, who knew I would travel the world?

JAY-Z: Yeah. Travel. Right. Exactly.

BK: What's that been like for you?

JAY-Z: It's all like an amazing ride, man. It's like, I see what happens if you really set your mind to do stuff. You know I set my mind to be here. I set my mind to be sitting right here and to be talking and be at this level of my career. And it happened for me. So I can honestly tell people from experience like if you put your mind to something that you really go after it, it could really happen for you. You know what I'm saying?

> Know what you're saying? I wrote it! I am highlighting the concept of tunnel vision, focus, and drive. There's a common concept from successful artists of putting in the work, pretty much all of my classic conversations have this mantra. If you put your mind to something and go after it, it could really happen for you. You're welcome. I kid...

BK: You know, obviously I got nothing but love for Jay-Z. You know, there's no doubt about that. You're on an amazing ride.

JAY-Z: Thanks man.

BK: Now with this amazing ride you can get a high profile, like obviously you got ups and downs. How have you handled the exact opposite of what we're talking about? I'm not talking about your shit that's going down right now. How do you deal with the quote unquote negativity?

JAY-Z: Right. God granted me the serenity to accept the things that I cannot change, you know what I'm saying? So I just accept the things that I can't change and I keep moving. I take it with a grain of salt. You know, I'm saying I can't stop people being negative towards me, or people from trying to do things to me, you know what I'm saying? I accept that I know I'm being judged by so many people, not everyone is gonna agree with what I have to say , you know? I'm judged by a whole lot of people and I know everyone can't love what I say, or what I do or what I represent, you know what I'm saying? I'm just here, I put myself out here, like, here, this is me, you know? It's a sin to judge people, you know, but [chuckles] I just could do what I do, man.

BK: If that's a sin, I'm telling you a lotta people breaking the law. [lots of laughter]

> That's my paraphrase of the song lyric, "If loving you is wrong, I don't wanna be right."

BK: You know, from day one you really haven't held back on saying stuff, you know, "the dissing" other rappers which has always been fine in hip hop.

JAY-Z: Right. That's what hip hop is built on. That's where I started, you know, I'm just cold crushing 'em having battles every day. That's what rap started as. That's what it is about going out [rapping] "I'm telling you. So I'm the best son." I didn't invent it.

BK: You started a few years back, which actually, you know now that it's been a few records, you can kind of look back to the initial rise. What was that like? How do you describe what that…

JAY-Z: I remember hearing the first time "Dead Presidents" from the first album got added to the radio. We was jumping up and down like we won the lottery or something. It was like, yeah, because it's about to happen. We felt like it was about to happen. And we just picked up steam. Then "Ain't No" came out the next record and it was goodbye. [chuckles]

BK: Goodbye, because I mean, the best example is my girlfriend, my fiancée you know, she still thinks Steely Dan and John Denver's cool. She knows "Ain't No." She knows it, she would sing it, she thought the hook was the funniest thing in the world and we'd sing it back to each other.

JAY-Z: Right. [chuckles]

BK: You know, talk about crossing, you know, a battle there.

JAY-Z: Yeah, that's what I'm talking about. A song so real it breaks all genders, all colors everywhere. Like people in London you know, singing that song. It just is crazy. That's what I'm talking about, making records that are so like about a subject and so real about a subject. It's ill for someone to say that but that's real, that really goes on.

BK: Hey, listen I sleep around but she still loves me a lot, you know no doubt.

JAY-Z: I mean, guys, let's just admit we're not the smartest strongest guys in the world you know. We're weak, weak in the flesh and we sometimes, we don't think with the proper brain.

> Ahhh, this was so long ago and there's no chance in hell that I would be singing again with that girlfriend, fiancée, who eventually became my wife, and then ex-wife. We both settled for plan B. This was just another example of how Jay kept it real, and that authenticity helped his music cross over to a larger audience. Mo' fans, mo' money. And what did he spend his money on in the year 2000?

BK: What's your medium extravagance? What's the one thing that you finally got a little coin on you, the one thing you just say, is it a car, a home, is it food?

JAY-Z: You know, I mean, with jewelry and things like that, I just have that. My goal is so far away like, on your way to your goal you have to pick up things that remind yourself that you're making some progress. I don't want people to think that I'm so much in love with these things, it's just things that I pick up on my way to show myself look,

I'm making progress. You know, it's temporary happiness. It's like tangible things. The thing that makes me most happy like, you know, I bought my moms a home. You know every boy's dream is that, that's every young boy's dream is they had bought their mom a home. So that was the most exciting thing for me.

BK: What she think of her baby?

> This is a clear example of "leading the witness" in the courts, or teeing up a softball question in entertainment journalism.

JAY-Z: She's in love. [chuckle] She's always been in love. But she's in love all over again. She calls me eight o'clock in the morning, often to read stuff that she read in the papers about me and stuff like that. Just excited, I love to see that.

BK: I asked you to touch a little bit on the future before in music. As far as the future future, let's just sum it up. Talk to me about where you want to be, what you want to be doing, whether it's the movies, whether you want...

JAY-Z: I want to do it all and I want to leave a legacy. Like I want to leave a business when I finally have kids, for my nephews, Dame's kids, and things like that. So they could grow into money. You know, us as Black people, we don't really get the, you know, a lot of white people, you know, they just get to grow into money you know what I'm saying? Everyone doesn't come from money. I want them to just come and have a business, something that they could go to school and learn more about, you know what I'm saying? That's my father's business right there and I want to take care of it. And I want to run a business like he would, and I want to leave it for my son.

BK: Or maybe they don't want to which is even better, giving them an option. Like my father, I could have gone into the meat business. I don't want to go into the meat business. I had that option, no thank you dad.

JAY-Z: Yeah, right right right. Exactly, yeah, right. That's great.

Jay was on team BK, and the feeling was mutual—and still is.

He was one of my last interviews of my initial decade run. I stayed in his universe by promoting some of his projects through the media circuses I had been accustomed to producing. I was thrilled when he showed up at my Radio Music Awards event in Las Vegas, and I've got the photo to prove it.

The last time we hugged it out in person was in 2005 when Jay introduced Rihanna to the music industry at a private event in Santa Monica. Supporting her felt like supporting him—a small way to champion his vision and the artists he believed in. I always knew he'd leave a lasting mark on music and culture, but I didn't fully see the "mogul in the making" trajectory—not being that close to his inner circle.

To get some perspective, I asked my best friend, Motti Shulman, who worked with Jay early on at Def Jam, promoting many of his records. Did he ever think "hova" would become the Roc Nation rock star and mega-mogul he is today? Without missing a beat, Motti said, "Most definitely." He knew. Everyone knew.

I'm beyond grateful for the conversation with Jay-Z, knowing he's since gone on to achieve so many of his dreams and built a legacy that will inspire generations. Before I left the interview, I asked him to sign an album poster for me, and he inscribed it, "To BK (Brooklyn)..." For years, that poster remained rolled up in storage, forgotten and slowly deteriorating. Then came the pandemic. While going through my archives I rediscovered it and memories came flooding back. Today, the framed poster hangs proudly by my garage door. Every time I leave my house to tackle the world, I glance at it and hum "allow me to reintroduce myself."

JAY-Z
...LIFE AND TIMES OF S. CARTER
DEC. 28TH

To B.K
Thats my Hometown
Roc
Jay

HERE'S THE INFAMOUS
BK BROOKLYN POSTER

YOU'RE ABOUT TO WITNESS A DYNASTY LIKE NO OTHER...

montell jordan

2 Barry - peace & respect 2 you - thanx 4 the excellent interview! continued success -
Montell Jordan

Photo Credit: TONY CUTAGAR

EPILOGUE
WITH MONTELL JORDAN

It was June 1st, 1995—one of those career-highlight days I didn't fully appreciate until years later. I was at Def Jam's West Coast offices, sitting across from their first R&B artist, Montell Jordan. His breakout single, "This Is How We Do It," had just spent seven weeks at number one. It's good to be the king.

What I remember most? Montell's warmth, his height (6'8")—and the fact that he was the only artist who ever both rapped and sang to me in the same interview.

And since this book profiles many of the defining voices of '90s Hip Hop and R&B, Montell has to be part of the story. After all, he was one of the first artists to blend both styles on a debut album.

So, I will make it quick and painless for you—the same thing I told present-day Pastor Montell Jordan when I emailed him, asking if he'd be up for a second interview—30 years later.

BK: YOU are literally the reason for me doing some version of classic conversations. I was digitizing your interview over Covid and my daughter walked by and said, "Who's that?" And I said, "You won't know who that is, it's Montell Jordan." She looks at me and she says "Of course I know Montell Jordan, 'This Is How We Do It.' Come on." And I was just like, I love her. And then I love YOU!

MJ: Yeah. Well, that's good parenting right there first of all. So, congratulations to you [chuckle].

BK: You've had more than enough time to kind of look back at that era of the craziness and you going through it, have you been able to sum it up?

MJ: I look at it as "grace" man. It literally for me is God's grace. There are lots of artists and lots of songs…I'm from an era where on a Tuesday you went to the store to see who dropped on Tuesday. And that was very, very different from today, where I could drop a new song in the next 30 minutes if I wanted to. And so I call it "grace" that 30 years later, we could be talking about a song that not only entered the music industry, but it actually became a part of music.

BK: When I was younger, I used to have to ask all artists, including yourself, about the '60s being a special decade for music, because I was doing a '60s radio show too. But now, as I'm older and I'm looking back, I feel like the '90s were a special decade for hip hop and R&B. Am I wrong?

MJ: No, I would have to agree. I think that even for me, the '60s still gave me some incredible things that I loved about music. '70s was cool, you know, '70s was some good stuff. I really love the '80s. I have an affection and an affinity for the '80s, probably even more than the '60s, because the '80s is what started shaping me with pop music and R&B music kind of crossing these lines.

These are the Prince and the Michael Jackson era, and the Cyndi Lauper and Madonna. So for me, I think the '60s was more for my mom and dad, the '80s more so for me. And now the '90s for me. Even where we are right now, I still find the '90s music, R&B, hip hop making a baby for the first time. I think that is where the sweet spot of music collides for me.

BK: I love it because I have 12 artists in this book. You kind of know all of them. If I say the name, just give me the first thing that comes to mind, okay?

[Montell agrees]

BK: Vanilla Ice.

MJ: Friend. I tour with him. We do "I Love the '90s Tour" and all these years later, he headlines tours and stages across the world.

BK: Second artist, you know as well, very closely, Boyz II Men.

MJ: Oh. First word that comes to mind was, oh, legends. Legends, modern day Temptations, modern day Spinners, Four Tops, modern day R&B group, lifetime group.

BK: TLC.

MJ: Oh, sweethearts. I miss Left Eye, love Chilli. Great, great women. I've been out with them touring over the past couple of years as well. These are peers and sisters. I think I would say "sisters" is my word there.

BK: There's one, I don't want to scare you, but his name's R. Kelly. He's in my book because he's a classic conversation. Because when I interviewed him, he was unbelievable. Talent wise, you can't really deny anything about this man.

MJ: You can't talk about the '90s without talking about Robert. But the word that immediately came to my mind was "tragedy." Tragedy that the genius of music could not supersede the infallible appetites of humanity. And that's very, very difficult.

BK: You ARE a minister…Toni Braxton.

MJ: Sultry. Sultry. To me, it was after Anita Baker. To me, she's filled that spot for me of modern-day Anita Baker.

BK: One of my favorite interviewees is a guy named Will Smith. He just knew how to interview. But when I say Will Smith to you back in the '90s…

MJ: If you say Will Smith to me back in the '90s, I think "clean" for whatever reason, you know. I came out of South Central, LA—Boyz n the Hood, Eazy-E, Ruthless Records, even Def Jam. Like the stuff that I was listening to, there had to be an element of the rawness of language in the street or whatever. And Will had the ability to communicate so clearly and tell stories that I could play in front of my mom.

BK: And that's what he said, so next one. I interviewed MC Hammer during his Funky—I don't know if you remember—during his "pumps and a bump" phase. But you must have been…

MJ: I mean, Hammer was king at that, at that time period. Like touring, the traveling, the modern day fanfare of having 30 people on stage and like, he was larger than life.

BK: Unbelievable. Here's another one that I was

fortunate to interview. Aaliyah. I interviewed her for her debut album. Gone too soon.

MJ: Yeah. Once again, I don't want to use the same word "tragedy." But, I think when it comes to Aaliyah [long pause for reflection]…

BK: No, I hear you.

MJ: I mean, I'm a word guy, and so I'm trying to find a word that fits. One word that…for her leaving— premature. Premature would be my word.

BK: The other person I put in the book, only because I love him so much, and he's technically not '90s hip hop and R&B. Although he won a Grammy in 1991, Luther Vandross.

MJ: Mmmmm. Luther…icon. I love Luther. I loved his voice. It was—there's pieces of his story, of not feeling loved, that drove him into some different spaces that are really painful to hear. But, for me, his voice and his persona is iconic to me.

BK: Yeah. There's only three left. One was, I believe your labelmate LL Cool J. I got to interview him a bunch of times back in the day.

MJ: G.O.A.T.

BK: G.O.A.T.? It's like drop it, you're done.

MJ: Listen, I love hip hop, and I love the whole Jay-Z, Biggie, Nas, Kanye blah blah blah. LL's the G.O.A.T.

BK: Missy, Missy Elliott. I describe her as an "original," but I don't know what you would say about Missy.

MJ: I would say—I don't think it's a fair word, but I would say "alien." For me, as in, meaning in a supernatural space. She's a creative musical alien that to me is just something that is foreign to what we know humanly possibly musically. So yeah.

BK: Still, I mean, she actually got into the Rock and Roll Hall of Fame…it's crazy.

MJ: Originator. If "alien" is a bad word, I'd say "originator."

BK: My last is another labelmate Jay-Z. If you would have told me that he was going to become a mogul, I didn't get it. Did you?

MJ: Yeah, yeah. I think the word immediately that comes to mind when you say Jay-Z is "industry." Like to me, he represents the overall like, if I have dreams, you know, sometimes and Jay-Z, in some way he's affiliated or associated in a dream that I'm having. I know that represents something about the business to me, about music, about something around that entire world.

So even though I can call "LL" the G.O.A.T., to me, the compartmentalization of that would be Jay-Z, to me represents the industry.

BK: Thank you man.

MJ: I appreciate you. Make sure y'all tip your cup and throw your hands up. One for your man Montell. All right?

All right indeed. That is how we do it. Sorry, had to. I always knew songs from the artists I profiled would live on, but I think their stories, these stories have a life of their own. Maybe, maybe not. But a brother can dream.

THANKS FOR LISTENING!

ABOUT THE AUTHOR
BARRY KRUTCHIK

Barry Krutchik is an entertainment journalist and creative force behind some of the most memorable audio programming and live events in pop culture. He has interviewed over 2,000 artists across music, film, and television, capturing candid moments with some of entertainment's most influential names.

Born in Brooklyn, raised in North Miami Beach, and based in Los Angeles, Barry still wrestles daily with his inner East Coast–West Coast rivalry — though unlike the legendary rap battles, his usually ends with a good laugh and a great story.

www.ingramcontent.com/pod-product-compliance
Lightning Source LLC
Chambersburg PA
CBRC091135130526
44582CB00034B/171